YOU INFLUENCE THE WORLD

AN OUTLINE OF HOW TO GET
AND MANAGE DIVINE MENDING

PAUL RAYMOND

YOU INFLUENCE THE WORLD

AN OUTLINE OF HOW TO GET

AND MANAGE DIVINE MENDING

PAUL RAYMOND

Foreword

You Influence the world; subtitled an outline of how to get and manage divine mending; shows the author delving into the reception and administration of healing. This book is timely because many people are looking for healing and they have almost forgotten that they have a role/part to play. Yes, the dimension that healing has taken in the recent past is such that requires a reminder and deeper emphasis on the role we must play, rather than moving from place to place, crusade to crusade, or pastor to pastor.

There is no doubt that we need healing in our world, physically, spiritually, and psychologically; and this is because humanity has been grappling with so many calamities both natural and man-made. However, one must begin that journey to wholeness by first realizing the role to be played in receiving God's healing and obtaining same for others; this means that, you must know what it is you have to do as a sick person seeking healing and what you ought to do as a family member, friend or minister in helping people receive healing and transformation.

This book has carefully elaborated on the roles that you can play and that of ministers, with good scriptural exposition on practice always to sustain healing, reasons why people lose their healing, and some healing scriptures which you will find a treasure to help you.

Other discussions in this book are rich and concise.

I am confident that this book will be of great help to many, and I invite you to take advantage of the richness it offers to bless yourself and others.

Fr. Musa Dogmo Sebastine

If It Wasn't For You

I give thanks to the Almighty Father, for His infinite mercy and goodness upon my life, family and ministry. I am grateful to my priests for every spiritual support towards me and this work, especially, Rev. Fr. Musa Dogmo Sebastine, I appreciate all my mentors and mentees. Thank you so much Mr. Anthony Ashibuogwu, Bro. John Udenenwu, Bro. Emmanuel Nneji, Mrs. Onah Lawretta and to you, that is reading this book. May God bless you all for your efforts and labour of love in Jesus' name, Amen.

Dedication

This treasure of a book is dedicated to *Yahweh Rapha*, the greatest Healer of all ages.

Remarks

It was St. Augustine who said that God has made us without our collaboration yet can't save us without our participation. It subsequently intends that, God can't simply mend us without our dynamic cooperation. The expression of God in Mathew 7:7 says, ask, look for and thump, for the people who ask get, the individuals who look for find and to the individuals who thump, the entryway will be opened to them.

The writer of this book has demonstrated for certain that for God to mend us, be it genuinely, profoundly, monetarily, mentally, and in any case, He wants our participation. We are the central heroes of such recuperating, hence, have a functioning part to play for us to accept our mending.

St. James likewise says that confidence without work is dead. We might have the confidence enough to accept our recuperating yet in the event that that confidence isn't shown or set in motion, it is on par with nothing. It accordingly intends that as devotees, we play a functioning part to play for us to get and support our mending from God. This book consequently is a rich piece for all professors deprived of God's recuperating and profound sustenance. I subsequently prescribe it to all with practically no booking.

Fire up. Fr. Terfa Lortyom.

Catholic Bishopric of Jalingo Taraba State, on secondment to Kontagora See, Niger State, Nigeria.

Table of content

Cover page

Foreword

If it wasn't for you

Dedication

Remarks

Presentation

Section One

GOD'S JOB

Section Two

THE JOB OF A CLERGYMAN

Section Three

THE JOB OF THE DEBILITATED

Section Four

DIVINE WELLBEING - YOUR REDEMPTIVE RIGHT

Section Five

DIVINE MENDING IS OUR REDEMPTIVE RIGHT

Section Six

SATAN IS THE CREATOR OF INFECTION

Section Seven

You Influence the world

THE MOST EFFECTIVE METHOD TO SUPPORT YOUR RECUPERATING

Section Eight

YOU SHOULD NOT BE MET EMPTY

References

You Influence the world

PRESENTATION

The principal thing I would like us to note here, concerning great wellbeing; divine mending and how to support it, is that no one can get heavenly recuperating without confidence (Jews 11:6). Furthermore, to get heavenly recuperating, one requires collaboration with the beauty of God by submissively doing precisely exact thing God charges us to do in His promise" (Luke 17:11-14), For instance, when one goes to the Clinic to see a specialist, the person makes it a point to the theater for conclusion, after which one gets the solutions and in compliance accepts the drug as recommended by a trained professional or an expert. Be that as it may, a few of us need to get heavenly recuperating from Yahweh Rapha, who is the maker of the relative multitude of educators, subject matter experts and specialists, without having their own influence to get it going. In the expressions of Priest David Oyedepo "On the off chance that you are not sufficiently extended, you can't spread successfully". We should quit wishing that things will change and begin acting. The time has come to act since it is said that "Assuming wishes were ponies, hobos will ride".

Darling, as you will find in this little book, 'mending arrangements' have been flawlessly and supernaturally made, yet conditions to get and support it, is through human collaboration with the heavenly beauty. In 1Corinthians 3:6 we see obviously that Paul assumed the part of planting, Apollos assumed his own part of watering the very plant that Paul had planted, while God the creator of life, caused what was planted and watered to develop and develop.

Discussing wishes, there is a fundamental thing in the existence of Jesus to gain from. In Matthew 26:36-46, when His service and mission to save mankind, was at its pinnacle; He saw the agonies that He was going to go through and needed to think about His own will of not drinking from that cup of distress. In any case, on a doubt, He said no, never! 'Not my will or wish but rather the desire of my dad'. He left the internal witnesses and immediately moved into the enthusiasm room, where He truly anguished and worked in supplication; for solidarity to at long last have His impact to save and accommodate man back to his creator. Upon man's fall, the equity arrangement of God expected that man's transgression be made up for, at the completion of time, Jesus Christ willingly set out his life to reclaim man (Phil 2:5-8; Jn 10:18; Lady 4:4-5; Jews 10:7-10). It is significant we comprehend that Jesus' expectation for man's salvation was never about humankind alone; He was additionally with his activity, satisfying the desire of the Godhead. In Gethsemane, He implored until his perspiration were thick in the comparability of drops of blood.

Once in a while we want to design ourselves after other extraordinary men. Actually, it is significant we pose inquiries to grasp the mysteries of their prosperity and progress. Every one of the Commanders that were significantly utilized by God, would they say they were individuals of wishes alone? Could it be said that they were not individuals of activity who will persevere relentlessly in playing their parts to help out God in his motivations completely?

In the event that the one who was deserted at the pool of Bethsaida by his family, companions and well-wishers didn't help out Jesus and had his own impact of getting his mat, as taught, he could never have accepted his mending. We excessively can do likewise and be liberated from that appalling story. We ought to always remember that "the people who sow in tears will procure in euphoria. He, who goes out sobbing, conveying the seeds for planting, will unquestionably return in the future with euphoria, conveying his piles" (Song 126:5). It is a pity that when certain individuals are being urged to have confidence and have their influence when looked by affliction(s), they deny saying that 'what is composed is composed'. They neglect to comprehend that regardless of the degree of wrongs, which Satan through his representatives might have composed into their redemptive freedoms [of mending and great health], it tends to be adjusted. So feel free to make the important penances [of having your impact out of affliction] (Isaiah 38:1-5).

Satan is a pioneer; he is genuinely exploiting certain individuals' otherworldly chilliness to control their wellbeing and mending. Assuming they just know this; and know that heavenly recuperating and great strength of both psyche and body, is their redemptive right, they will ascend from their sleep, and genuinely keep watch to safeguard their heavenly legacy. In 1 Ruler 21:3, Naboth shared with

You Influence the world

Ruler Ahab, "the Master preclude me that I ought to give the legacy of my dads to you". Obliviousness they say is a sickness. On the off chance that we really get it and consistently recall what Jesus went through, to recover us, we won't be for all time ablaze and ever give Satan a traction to haggle over our legacy. The day Esau was to procure and pay for his skeptical indiscreet demeanor, he shouted out with an incredible and very harsh cry, and asked his dad as subsequently, "Favor me, even me likewise, gracious my dad" (Beginning 27:34). Assuming that we neglected to be delicate and enough safeguard our redemptive privileges, let us be additionally prepared to mourn like Esau when it will be past the point of no return.

Satan is really the main entertainer behind every possible kind of malevolence and devilishness that happens today, around us as well as on the planet at large. He is the creator of ailment and illnesses. He is continually ready to drive you extremely quick into transgression, affliction, need, discouragement lastly annihilate (kill) you. At the point when we choose to help out God; our producer and deliverer, who is more anxious to pardon, to recuperate and to reestablish us back to greatness, Satan loses his grasp on us and we are liberated.

Rather than taking your life the manner in which your foes expect or want, you will astound them by finishing the manner in which your producer initially planned from days of yore.

> *"The Master invalidates the direction of the countries; He makes the considerations and plans of individuals ineffectual. The guidance of the Master stands always, the contemplations and plans of His heart through all age [Blessed, prosperous, and inclined toward by God] is the country whose God is the Ruler, individuals whom He has picked as His own legacy" (Song 33:10-12).*

One of the advantages of profound sharpness is that it empowers one to be in control and have dominance over crafted by the tissue. What's more, when one carries on with a very much focused life, it will at this point not be an issue for the individual to remain away or decline absolutely from way of life designs that don't ensure a good outcome.

At the point when we outfit the arrangements of God (in His promise) and have our existences as He wills, the issue of getting our wellbeing and mending supported will never again be. Certain individuals have extraordinary energy and excitement, which causes them to take part in physical and otherworldly activities that can convey them from dilemmas, notwithstanding, they miss the mark in carrying on with their existences as God wills, accordingly their lives are messed up, causing them to endure and regret like God is has become Baal who can't help or safeguard its admirers. Indeed, when our life is all together; we will be aware, what to eat and when to eat it, when and how to ask, what and how to study, when and how to quick, when to participate in actual activity or preparing; like going for a stroll or going to the exercise center and when not to; when and how to offer oneself a reprieve and rest.

Immediately, recollect that we have yet one life to live, and remember in all your getting, to get understanding and astuteness which is the chief thing (Adage 4:7).

Petition

My Master and my God, your statement expresses that by books, the eyes of Daniel were opened to be aware, that the seventy years of his kin's subjugation were finished (Daniel 9:2). Father, you are the Divine force of Daniel who never shows signs of change, through the assistance of the Essence of God, give me the effortlessness to peruse this little book on recuperating, and as I read it, let my eyes be opened to see, comprehend and have the specific influence and job, that is expected of me in my life and service, through Christ our Ruler So be it.

SECTION ONE

GOD'S JOB

In this section, I will show us cautiously from the sacred writings, a portion of the different jobs, that God played in the existences of many individuals that needed redemption, recuperating and get through.

In his book **"God: Find His personality"** Bill Brilliant makes sense of exhaustively a portion of the qualities of God, one of which was love.

I concur with Bill since quite possibly of the best job that our dad and creator (otherwise called Yahweh Rapha) played towards the reclamation and mending of humanity is surrendering His main generated child. A sacrificial gift to and for mankind, simply roused by agape love. In section 53 of the book of Isaiah, the prophet frames exhaustively, the significant part or job that the Godhead played to save humanity from the misdirection and persecution of Satan. After the fall of man (Gen 3), man was ill-fated to never-ending destruction, however for God, who sent His main sired child. The child of man didn't come to annihilate men, however to save them" (Luke 9:56).

> *"For it is unimaginable for the blood of bulls and goats to remove sins. Subsequently, when Christ appeared on the scene, he said, penances and contributions you have not wanted, however a body you have arranged for me, in consumed contributions and sin contributions you have taken no joy. Then, at that point, I said, see, God, I have come to do your will, gracious God" (Jews 10:4-7).*

At the point when the Congregation was conceived, Satan through his representatives promised to eradicate the Congregation through oppressions and killing of Christians. He didn't realize that mistreatment rather obliterating the congregation, would assemble and fortify it (Mat 16:18).The early church father, Tertullian is credited to have said "The blood of the saints is the seed of the congregation". When Lord Herod Agrippa I, the grandson of Herod the extraordinary killed James the sibling of John by sword and saw that what he did satisfied the Jews, he captured Peter as well. Be that as it may, the Congregation never nodded off, they rather held fast in supplication and God answered and played the accompanying parts.

He sent His holy messenger and the holy messenger who addressed God in this occasion, showed up in the jail cell with light so that Peter might be able to see. The holy messenger tapped Peter as an afterthought and awakened him and expressed, "Get up rapidly" Dearest, it is vital we note here and not fail to remember in a rush that God through His holy messenger didn't accomplish for Peter in jail, what Peter could accomplish for himself. At the point when God trained Peter through His heavenly messenger to get up rapidly, the two chains around his wrist were still on him, yet when Peter answered by having his own influence, the evil, Herodic chains around him immediately tumbled off his wrist. Moreso, the holy messenger told Peter, attach your belt and put on your shoes and he did as such. Then, at that point, he told him, fold your shroud over you and follow me. Peter went out and followed him and didn't understand that what was befalling him was genuine. The sacred text expressed that Peter thought he was seeing a dream (Acts 12:1-9).

Darling, God plays a part to play towards our opportunity, mending and forward leap, nonetheless, He won't ever accomplish for us that which we can accomplish for ourselves. Our God is awesome and composed. At the point when the holy messenger of God had not shown up or showed up in the jail cell where Peter was, the entire spot was in absolute murkiness and God through His heavenly messenger never tried to awaken Peter, since he won't see or have his impact out of the jail without light.

> *"Again Jesus addressed them, saying, I'm the radiance of the world. Whoever follows me won't ever stroll in murkiness however will have the radiance of life" (John 8:12).*

God can't and won't ever accomplish for any man or lady how the individual can help him/herself. At the point when the holy messenger of God showed up in the jail to help Peter out of his issue, the light from paradise that followed the holy messenger scattered the murkiness and the holy messenger woke Peter since he was resting and couldn't play out any obligation while snoozing. It was after Peter awakened that the evil, Herodic chain tumbled from him, and the heavenly messenger educated him to get up and wear his belt and shoes, put on his shroud and follow him. These are jobs that Peter just did for himself.

It is vital we note that God could never have assumed Peter's part for him. Herod needed to kill Peter as he had killed James the sibling of John by the sword. Yet, when the devotees had their influence, through interminable extremist petitions, God interceded by sending His holy messenger to safeguard Peter (that is God's part). The fact that kept Peter alive makes him the one. His blessing and shrewdness upon Peter was working empowering him to get up rapidly, put on his shroud, wear his belt and shoes and follow the holy messenger out of the jail.

JESUS' JOB

In my office, clients regularly refer to me as "Oga" (ace), particularly when they maintain that I should take care of them on a specific issue. Furthermore, each time individuals address or call me ace, similar to a joke, I will continuously let them know that I am not the expert here, that the expert is **JESUS**. Despite the fact that individuals or clients use to see my constant statement or reaction to them each time they call me ace as an approach to facilitating pressure or telling of wisecracks. They wouldn't grasp that my statement of Jesus as the expert, is a calling or announcement that emerges from my inward most heart.

WHO THEN IS A MASTER

Longman Word reference of contemporary English characterizes an expert as Ruler or an individual who has general power over others. The expert in this setting is Jesus. He is the Chief. What's more, the supervisor is an individual who is in control. Julius isn't the expert; the expert is Jesus. He is the ruler. What's more, a ruler is an individual who leads or oversees. A ruler is likewise an individual who practices territory or controlling control over others.

You Influence the world

Jesus is Ruler, and as a co-maker with the Dad and the Essence of God, He knows the materials you and I were made of. As the Ruler and expert, He has authority over our lives and not Satan and ailment of any sort. Cherished, I maintain that you should strikingly tell Satan and that affliction, that Jesus is your Chief and consequently has each privilege to be always responsible for your life elements and not Satan and ailment. Offspring of God, do you have any idea that as a ruler, that Jesus manages all over the place? Along these lines, it doesn't make any difference where we are presently or everything certain individuals might have said to us, and we acknowledged and began viewing ourselves as such. Might be we went to see our clinical Specialist and after assorted analysis we were insistently informed that our case is confounded and in this manner has no clinical cures?

In 2007, my tutor had a debilitated call that was extremely earnest and welcomed me to go with him to the individual's home. Also, in no time before we petitioned God for that individual, we guided him and found that the issue that nearly driven him to loss of motion was as consequence of dread imparted in him, for the sake of disclosure or prediction by his righteous man so to say. In the event that not the benevolence of God that was immediately shown in the existence of this individual, in the wake of advising and supplications, Satan would enjoy taken benefit of that wrong evil prediction and put him in never-ending desolation. From the encounters I have had up to this point, in my little long periods of administration in God's grape plantation, I need to emphatically pursue, that we ought to be extremely cautious and adequately knowing, to understand what we ought to acknowledge to consume into our framework or subliminal psyche for the sake of what I call; negative, self-evident and wrong sort of messages or predictions, that people who might not have stood by sufficient in that frame of mind of God, are spreading near. I don't have the foggiest idea who might be perusing this book at the present time, and what your encounters in the past were like? Have you fallen modest in the possession of the specialists of haziness, letting you know lie for the sake of God? Dread not and have confidence in what God says in His composed word (Joshua 1:9).

Adored, don't be apprehensive and ensure you don't concern yourself, for stress invalidates confidence, petition and wonder. What's more, every superfluous trepidation and stress is a proof that one doesn't really accept that that God can deal with us. Jesus is a companion and a ruler who governs all over the place and in each situation. In (Sirach 24:7) the sacred text records that Jesus is searching for a spot to settle. Furthermore, may I likewise rapidly advise us, that as a ruler, Jesus has domain, power and command over Satan and disorders, everything being equal? It is on the grounds that Jesus loves, and enthusiastically thinks often about all that concerns you and I, that made Him to descend from paradise to the earth, to show us the correct way, and from the earth to the cross where all our obligation was paid for. His excursion from the cross to the grave and from the grave to the sky is a confirmation, that He manages all over the place.

As the expert and ruler, nothing can stop Jesus, from venturing into any circumstance and spot He wants, not even the difficulty in our lives right presently can stop Him.

> *"After He came back to life, when it was evening on that day, the principal day of the week, and the entryways of the house where the devotees had met were locked inspired by a paranoid fear of the Jews, He came and remained among them and said, harmony be with you"(John 20:19).*

Jesus is the Sovereign of Harmony, and in this way, assuming there is any aspect of our lives that is by and by in emergencies, simply welcome Him with confidence and perceive how our tears of distress will be transformed into bittersweet tears bliss.

Any entryway of leap forward, prompting our recuperating marvels that was closed by Satan and his representatives can limit men and their clinical sciences, and not Jesus, the expert, who controls all over the place.

After the demise of Jesus, the followers were totally damaged. They nearly lost trust and ended up being confounded. They didn't be aware at that period, where and whom to go to, on the grounds that the Expert of the relative multitude of bosses, the Educator of the relative multitude of educators, the Ruler of the multitude of masters, the Stone of ages, the antiquated of days, the Lion of the clan of Judah, the brilliant and morning star, the expectation of the miserable, the person who Peter expressed to in one event in good news of (John 6:68) "Ruler, to whom will we go to? You [alone] have the expressions of everlasting life [you are our just hope]" is mysteriously absent. In that condition of problem, the main thing that crossed the personalities of the witnesses to do, was to head inside and lock themselves up. In any case, their lord, who is the top, all things considered, who held imprisonment hostage and gave gifts to men, entered their miserable circumstance with confirmation of "harmony accompany you". A reassuring assertion, a mending word which reinforced and conveyed them immediately, from dread and reestablished their mental fortitude and concentration.

> *"After this there was a celebration of the Jews, and Jesus went up to Jerusalem. Presently in Jerusalem by the sheep Entryway there is a pool, brought in Hebrew Bethzatha, which has five porticoes. In these lay many invalids - visually impaired, weak and deadened. One man was there who had been sick for 38 years. When Jesus saw him lying there and realize that he had been there quite a while, he shared with him, 'Would you like to be made well? The wiped out man responded to him, 'Sir, I have nobody to place me into the pool when the water is worked up; and keeping in mind that I am advancing, another person ventures down in front of me. Jesus shared with him, stand up, go for your mat and stroll.' on the double the man was made well. Also, he took up his mat and started to walk. Now that day was a time of rest. Thus, the Jews shared with the one who was relieved, 'It is the time of rest; conveying your mat" (John 5:1-10 isn't legitimate)."*

It is extremely agonizing to be wiped out and have nobody to deal with you. The wiped out powerless man in the pool of Bathzatha we read his story in the above sacred text, would have stayed there unendingly in hopelessness, if Jesus, the man I bring in my local language "Ogadagidi" (Strong God) won't ever appear. Jesus realize that this man, who was dreadfully and magnificently made by God, has been completely deserted by his companions and well-wishers for 38 great years. He additionally knew that disturbing this man's recuperating, that God Himself had proactively had His impact, by making the pool, and by sending in the people of altruism who filled the role of carrying the wiped out man to that pool in any case.

You Influence the world

Furthermore, having dissected the instance of this wiped out individual, Jesus basically finished up inside Him, that the main person that played not had his influence, all things considered is Him; and this made Him to go to the man and shared with him, man, take up your mat and go. I don't have the foggiest idea who is perusing this book at the present time, however in the event that you are debilitated and have burned through all you have. Your family, companions and well-wishers have likewise given their all to assist you with getting up to your feet once more but the disorder continued to challenge arrangements. Cherished, my guidance for you is to connect with Jesus, remain with Him and quit depending on what tissue can offer you. He will appear time permitting, particularly, when the insight about your mending and advancement will carry magnificence to God's realm and all out disgrace to Satan and every one of his representatives. Also, in particular, when He appears, don't be embarrassed to show Him precisely where and how your 'Lazarus' was covered. Thus, He can without much of a stretch order your dead 'Lazarus' to reawaken. There is no addition saying the truth today is that many are having various types of difficulties. The 'dead Lazarus' of Mr. A, probably won't be something very similar with Mr. B. Certain individuals are genuinely OK however are extremely debilitated in a profound way. Some are in a genuine way OK, and yet inwardly, intellectually and mentally debilitated. As far as some might be concerned, it is marriage, finance, occupation, profession and medical affliction.

Petition

God the Dad, God the Child, and God the Essence of God, you are great in sacredness, unfortunate in applauds, you are the Rose of Sharon, the Lily of the valley, my stone and my defender. I thank you kindly, for the brilliant job that you played, and the arrangements you have made to liberate me from subjugation of transgression that can open entryways and give fallen angel admittance to go after me. For the sake of Jesus Christ, I get elegance, to have my own influence and job, out of transgression, ailment and devilish abuse of any sort So be it. Father, for the sake of Jesus Christ, and by the force of the Essence of God, I come against any satanic bolts,

that was shot against my family, marriage, funds, wellbeing, work and vocation in Jesus' name So be it.

SECTION TWO

THE JOB OF A CLERGYMAN

Who is a clergyman? someone might inquire. Basically, a priest in this setting is that individual who addresses God here on the planet. He is that modest individual, who has gone through the quarry and different cycles of development by their creator. Such an individual is called and completely prepared to act as a channel of gift to God's kin. A priest is an individual, who knows God, complies, loves and practices His words, in any event, when it harms. A pastor is likewise an individual, who shows individuals the methods of God and urges them to cherish Him (Judges 7:17-18). The person in question is an individual, who is prepared to battle unafraid, blunders and pessimistic circumstances, in the existences of God's kin with what God said in His composed word. A clergyman is an individual, who is consistently prepared to move when God says move and stops when God says stop. The person in question is an individual, who stays within the sight of God, contingent completely upon Him, since Jesus expressed "cut off from me you can sit idle" (John 15:5).

Vital and worth saying clergymen are called by God. They convey God's presence and blessing. However, they are not God. They know to some degree, however God knows it all. They have constraints. Existence can get them abandoned, yet God in each feeling of thinking is limitless. The priests are people of God, and not Divine force of people. They live in similar society and urban communities where others reside. They eat as others do. The impact of ecological impact makes them to endure somewhat, what others in their current circumstance endure too.

In Imprint 16:20 the sacred text plainly says that when the messengers spoke about the gospel to individuals, that God affirmed their message with signs and ponders. Accordingly, in the event that the witnesses didn't have their impact of proclaiming of the gospel in any case, God could not have possibly had His own impact of affirming what was being taught. I need to praise my kindred priests in God's grape plantation, who are effectively working for God and with God. Congrats, troopers of Christ; for keeping the fire consuming. Nonetheless, may I likewise remind the pastors that despite the fact that it is genuine and really undisputable, that the redemptive work is a completed work, yet the clergymen actually have their parts to play? Taking everything into account, as a matter of fact, the pastors are the noticeable hands, the legs, the eyes and ears of God here on the planet. They ought to take note of that it is just when they act or have their impact, in some random situation that God will move, for power isn't dynamic until confidence is genuinely worked out.

THE JOB OF PROPHET EZEKIEL IN THE VALLEY OF DRY BONES

Prophet Ezekiel comprehended his call as a prophet, to such an extent that when God took him to the valley of dry bones for exploit, he immediately helped out his creator, had his influence and power changed hands; to such an extent that those bones that were exceptionally dry quickly reawakened. I believe you should be aware, that for Ezekiel to have answered rapidly to the direness of God's call and guidance, he above all else felt the strong presence of God. In Evangeli Nutiandi No. 75 (Proselytizing in the advanced world), the Catholic Church educates, "that the Essence of God, is the Key Specialist of Proselytizing." In this manner, it becomes basic, that for yourself and me to assume our parts towards the extraordinary errand of Proselytizing, which Mother Theresa of Calcutta of favored memory characterized as, "One having Christ in him/her and giving Him to other people." We should help out the Essence of God, making Him our companion to have the option to succeed in completing our inherent task precisely.

Assuming you read Ezekiel 37:1-10, you will figure out that, when Ezekiel felt the strong presence of God, he heard God obviously and explicitly pose him an inquiry about the condition of those dry bones, and how to change the irredeemable condition of those bones. God shared with him "prediction" and he forecasted, on the grounds that he comprehended that God can't bless a Prophet and descend from paradise to complete a task for which He had proactively blessed that prophet. Could it be said that you are a Prophet? What region do you imagine that God has called you to work in? For Ezekiel, his area of position by then was in the valley of dry bones. As a prophet, the work and the call of God upon you will be a lot more straightforward and useful, on the off chance that you find the special region of your calling. Is it true that you are a prophet? Kindly hear this, never attempt to mimic the example of another prophet since he is succeeding in his prophetic calling and style. No! this isn't permitted in the prophetic school, be unique. Yet, assuming you are among those that were called to deal with any lost causes or dry bones, go on, no real reason, the time has come to prophetically proclaim to any waste of energy around you, and quit wishing and holding up that things will change all alone. Might it be said that you are a Prophet? Gain from Prophet Ezekiel and don't attempt to talk when God has not spoken. No measure of tension, from individuals ought to allure you to make up a phony stuff to acquire impact and be praised by men. Keep in mind, that on the Day of atonement, you will give record of your stewardship to God alone, and not to any human.

THE JOB OF PETER AND JOHN AT THE WONDERFUL ENTRYWAY.

"One day Peter and John were going up to the sanctuary at the hour of petition, at three PM. What's more, a man faltering from birth was being conveyed in. Individuals would lay him everyday at the entryway of the sanctuary called the Delightful Door with the goal that he could want donations from those entering the sanctuary. At the point when he saw Peter and John going to go into the sanctuary, he asked them for offerings. Peter took a gander at him, as did John, and expressed, 'Take a gander at us.' And he fixed his consideration on them, hoping to get something from them. However, Peter said, 'I have no silver or gold, yet what I have I give you; for the sake of Jesus Christ of Nazareth, stand up and walk. Furthermore, he took him by the right hand and raised him up; and quickly his feet and lower legs were areas of strength for made. Hopping up, he stood and started to walk, and entered the sanctuary with them, strolling and lauding God" (Acts 3:1-8).

For Peter and John, going into the sanctuary at the 10th hour (3:00pm) to venerate is essential for their day to day daily schedule. On this specific day, quickly the weak man asked them for aid, which was the main part he could play;

You Influence the world

Peter and John made up their brains to have their own impact, involving the power for the sake of Jesus Christ. They were moved and became keen on the faltering man's situation when they saw that individuals who acquired the man to the sanctuary entryway had their influence. What's more, the faltering man himself has proactively had his influence and this made Peter to share with him, "take a gander at us, and he fixed his consideration upon them hoping to get something from them". Peter and John realize that the consideration of that faltering man has been profoundly redirected from now onward, indefinitely quite a while, into things that were not intended to bring him all out recuperating. Requesting silver and gold is great, yet that was not the very thing that God was offering the weak man that day, through the service of Peter and John.

As clergymen drew closer by individuals for guiding and supplications, asking and anticipating that God should mediate in their difficulties; we ought to gain from Peter and John, to appropriately recognize and guide their psyches to God who is Yahweh Rapha, and not to us the pastors. I have seen in various events, where individuals come for supplication looking for that which isn't God's psyche for them by then. Our obligation is to tell them, the brain of God and not what they need earnestly. All things considered, the faltering man never asked Peter and John for a supernatural occurrence; his craving was to have his pocket loaded up with cash.

THE JOB OF PROPHET ELISHA DURING THE STARVATION IN SAMARIA

The sort of starvation that visited individuals in the place where there is Samaria, was extraordinary. A portion of the Samaritans ate the bird's fertilizer, something detestable that shouldn't have entered their mouth notwithstanding the intensity of starvation. The shortage of food was destroying, to such an extent that a few ladies in the land lost their control and were not even embarrassed to answer to the lord that they were eating their kids to remain alive. That was the condition, at this point the ideal God who is omniscient currently established a prophet (Elisha) to take care of their concerns. Elisha sat in conversation for certain elderly folks in his home while individuals he was shipped off save were becoming baffled every day for absence of food. The lord of the land had his impact furtively. At the point when he heard that individuals currently eat individual people as food, he tore his dress in fury and put on rough clothing. At the point when the lord recalled that Elisha was near yet would not have his influence, he commanded Elisha with a capital punishment to assume his part as a prophet. Dr. Minister Paul Enenche would agree that that "the unwinding of a Prophet, is the dissatisfaction of individuals".

At the point when Elisha discovered that his life was currently at serious risk assuming he neglects to have his impact towards the disturbing food emergencies, he moved forward to his obligation and said, at this point tomorrow, the food emergencies will be finished.

SEVEN DIFFERENT WAYS BY WHICH HEAVENLY MENDING CAN BE GOTTEN OR MANAGED

Is it true or not that you are keen on assisting individuals with recuperating from sickness? Do you show some care for those needing heavenly mending? Is it safe to say that you are energetic over the debilitated? Do you have sympathy for them? Could it be said that you are anxious, each time you see individuals disappointed and truly enduring, in light of weakness? Have you been looking for the essence of God, petitioning God for recuperating blessing and shrewdness to help the wiped out? Like St. Paul, I'm not at all professing to have everything. Nor am I attempting to make a standard, no, never. In any case, what I'm going to impart to you here are seven different ways by which heavenly recuperating can be gotten or managed to the wiped out, these are not new or remarkable. They are somewhat, a disclosure I produced using my exploration and investigations of the sacred writings.

1. **Through individual petition:** In James 5:13, The missionary welcomes generally that are distressed to ask; and for the way that disorder is a kind of difficulty, any second affliction comes to go after you, one of the scriptural strategy or recipe to survive, overcome and leave it, is to stoop to God in extremist supplication of confidence by

and by. In Mark11:22-24 Jesus whose word is Definitely and So be it, finished up subsequently, "Really I tell you, assuming you share with this mountain, be taken up and tossed into the ocean, and in the event that you don't uncertainty in your heart, yet accept that what you say will happen, it will be finished for you. Along these lines, I tell you, anything you request in supplication, accept that you have gotten it, and it will be yours". I believe that you should comprehend what Jesus implied here. He never said, you should get what you asked in petition before you accept. No, that was not the very thing He implied here. He essentially said, when you implore, express no to uncertainty and accept that you have proactively gotten what you asked in petition, and it will show. At the point when Thomas showed elevated degree of uncertainty and would not acknowledge the message of different messengers that Jesus appeared to them, the Expert later returned and shared with Thomas accept and question no more; for favored are the people who have not yet seen (their recuperating wonder manifest), yet they accept it will appear in the closest future (accentuation mine). At the point when ten outcasts requested that Jesus mend them. He just shared with them, proceed to show yourselves to the minister; and the sacred writing records that they were mended on their way going to do what the Expert requested that they do. They were submissive and never questioned. That's what I know whether these outcasts were family of Thomas, who live in our general public today, they would have requested that Jesus ask and lay hands on them first, prior to sending them to the minister for affirmation of the marvel they were not even certain regardless of whether it will show.

2. Through laying of hands on the wiped out (Imprint 16:17-18): In 2009, we had a considerable petitioning heaven bunch, comprised of nine individuals who assemble in the Congregation each Monday to supplicate from 12 PM to the early hours (5:00am) of the day. As we accumulated to implore one evening, one of us came exceptionally wiped out and he needed to venture to every part of the following day

after our program, however to the greatness of God, the main thing we did before we began our ordinary supplication, was to lay hands on him and he was immediately recuperated. In the event that you give close consideration to Check's message as a feature of the signs that will follow the devotees (Imprint 16:17), you will comprehend that laying hands on the wiped out, is one of those strong weapons given to the adherents to dissipate disorder from individuals back to damnation.

3. **By the order of confidence:** "And Jesus told him if possible! Everything is feasible to him who accepts. Quickly the dad of the kid shouted out and said, I accept, assistance my unbelief! What's more, when Jesus saw that a group came running together, he reproached the messy soul, telling it, you moronic and hard of hearing soul, I order you, emerge from him, and at absolutely no point ever enter him in the future" (Imprint 9:23).

4. Through the expressed word (Mathew 8:8, John 4:50): One of the most breathtaking way individuals got recuperating in the service of Jesus was through His expressed word. At the point when the power or weapon of the verbally expressed word is involved or connected on a matter, reality isn't an issue. God will constantly respect His assertion over any deterrent (Jeremiah1:12)

5. Through the blessed piece of clothing (Imprint 6:56, Acts 19:11-12): When you hear me discuss the blessed article of clothing, I don't fundamentally imply that you ought to proceed to buy garments on the lookout, get back home and bless them with oil and begin offering it to individuals as an approach to getting their recuperating, actually no, not really. Rather, what I found in the service of Jesus and Paul was that when the debilitated reached out to their fabrics, they accepted their healings on the grounds that the recuperating blessing in their bones spilled over through the articles they wore. Very much like what occurred in the grave of Elisha (2 Rulers 13:20). Elisha was dead, covered and most likely neglected; yet the blessing he conveyed when

he was alive, was as yet secret in his bones hanging tight for the contact with any dead body to resurrect it. Darling, the blessing power is genuine.

6. I read an account of how Priest Idahosa, got a call from his family when he was in America for a campaign that his mom is dead. He let them know that it can't be imaginable on the grounds that God can't call his mom without telling him, in light of the fact that the last time he checked in the soul, his mom was as yet alive. They asked him, what will we do then, at that point? He advised them to keep her on his bed. They asked him, when are you returning, and he let them know in ten days' time when he completes his program. What's more, after ten days, when the campaign was finished, he returned and went directly to his room where his mom was saved dead for the beyond ten days and basically shared with her, "mom I'm back, sit up and give me water, and the mother answered, you are gladly received".

8. I likewise heard Diocesan David Oyedepo say in one of his messages that he got a call from his kin in the town to return home one day since his sibling had lost his mental soundness. The diocesan said that when he arrived at home, he essentially requested them to put his sibling inside his vehicle and let him see Satan that will follow him to his vehicle. Furthermore, when they put the debilitated man inside his vehicle his mental soundness returned. Blessing is critical and it has the effect. The void and weakness of Gehazi, a man who expected to convey the triple blessing of Elijah was genuinely uncovered when his lord (Elisha) sent him to proceed to bring up the dead offspring of the Shunamite lady back to life. Since you don't have it, doesn't mean it doesn't exist. Dearest, the force of God is genuine nevertheless working till tomorrow.

9. By respectfully playing out a demonstration of trust (2Kings 5:14, Luke 17:14): Setting your confidence in motion has a vital impact in bringing heavenly mending into moment sign. For example, on the off chance

that Naaman didn't act in confidence by dunking himself multiple times in the waterway as Elisha had coordinated, he could never have been restored of his sickness. In the event that we trust somebody enough to petition God for us, and during the time spent directing and supplication, the individual got propelled by God and let us know something to do which isn't a wrongdoing or unsafe, it is vital to comply. We might be exceptionally astounded by the result. The ten outsiders were savvy in submitting to the expert's order. That got their recuperating? They never contended with their creator. The expression of God helps us to "live with conviction, by focusing on the subtle". (2 Corinthians 5:7)

10. Through the blessing of the older folks (James 5:14-15): Today is miserable that our reality, never again have respect for their clerics, ministers and clergymen (the seniors). Rather, they have respect for mysterious and juju clerics. I realize that the explanation certain individuals never again have respect for certain clergymen of the gospel, is once in a while due to their way of life. In any case, that pastors in some cases fall in manners that make cultural embarrassments, shouldn't cause Satan to deny one of his/her right of recuperating, essentially in light of the fact that one might be admiring a clergyman rather than God. It is essential to guarantee that one is continuously focusing on Jesus (Hebrew 12:2). The Catholic Church instructs that the legitimacy or viability of a holy observance doesn't rely upon the way of life of the priest. However, this shouldn't likewise be a reason for a clergyman to fail to remember their call as a trooper of Christ and begin living like a normal non military personnel. Each pastor, as an issue of need, should lead their life, in away and way, that will cause individuals to appreciate Jesus in them, the desire for magnificence.

Petition

All strong and consistently living God, in appreciation for your call, and leniency in my life, I stand this second, to earnestly thank you, the old of

days, the alpha and omega, the brilliant and morning star, the unique advantage and the wonder laborer, for blessing and delegating me, among the clergymen of the gospel. For the sake of Jesus, and by the force of the Essence of God, I additionally thank you, for carrying this individual to yourself through me. As a prophet of effortlessness, I consequently stand in your name, to mediate for this individual. Father, in any capacity the person, may have trespassed against you, purposely or unconsciously, straightforwardly or by implication, that might remain as an obstruction or prevention to my request for that person, Ruler show kindness, Christ show kindness, Master show kindness. Much thanks to you father, for pardoning that person of any demonstration or hint of defiance, So be it.

Father, for the sake of Jesus, I stand in your promise, in Imprint 16:17, which says, that adherents will project out evil spirits in your name, and when they lay their hands on the debilitated, they will recuperate. In the name over each and every other name, I order any demon(s) that is answerable for the ailments and hardships, in the existence of this individual, to go out, presently forcibly and by fire in Jesus' name So be it. You soul of dread and uneasiness, you soul of dissatisfaction that prompts despondency, you soul of deferral, barrenness and unnatural birth cycles, you soul of sleep deprivation and craziness, you soul of lethargy that prompts prayerlessness, emerge and burst into flames, this moment in Jesus' name So be it.

SECTION THREE

THE JOB OF THE DEBILITATED

In this section, I plan to show you various jobs that people in book of scriptures times played to get mending and liberation from Yahweh Rapha, the best healer, everything being equal, who never turns down anybody who come to Him with outright confidence and genuineness?

What is confidence? In this unique situation, I need to characterize confidence, as my reaction to God's capacity. Confidence is seeing things with God's eyes. Confidence is my capacity to hear with God's ear. It is the powerful weapon, which has the ability to resurrect the dead. Without confidence it is totally difficult to if it's not too much trouble, get and do anything enormous or heavenly for the sake of God (Jews 11:6).

"It was confidence that held Enoch back from passing on" (Hebrews11:5). It was confidence that made Noah. It was confidence that made Abraham. It was confidence that made Isaac. It was confidence that made Jacob. It was confidence that made Joseph. It was confidence that made the guardians of Moses. It was confidence that made Moses. It was confidence that made individuals of Israel. It was confidence that made the Jericho wall fall. Confidence will likewise restore you. Assuming you cautiously think about the preliminaries that those referenced in the above sacred writings went through and later defeated leaning on an unshakable conviction; you will concur with me that regardless of whether Satan has shot a bolt of affliction at you, which is as of now gobbling you up, with the authentic weapon, that equivalent God who is the old of days can in any case restore you, since He is your creator and your mender. Have some time off from perusing and sing this melody, "You are here, moving here, I love you, I love you. You are here, moving in my life, I love you, I love you. Way producer, supernatural occurrence laborer, guarantee manager, light in the haziness, my God that is the sort of person you are"

Assuming it was confidence that held Enoch back from passing on, be have confidence offspring of God that no measure of affliction can kill you, you are unkillable when you have confidence in the God who held Enoch back from kicking the bucket and proclaimed that you are the apple of His eyes, unapproachable and strong (Zachariah 2:8). Regardless of how terrible the current situation with your wellbeing might appear, on the off chance that you can have the sort of confidence that Enoch had, you will definitely recuperate in light of the fact that in John 10:28 Jesus said, "on the grounds that I give them life, they won't ever die; and nobody can grab them from me". Offspring of God your life is genuinely concealed in Christ (Colossians 3:3).

The primary job that any wiped out individual needing heavenly mending ought to play as we will find in this part is the capacity to accept without questioning, in the truth of God's power and presence to recuperate and contact him.

Is it safe to say that you are debilitated? What have you up to about it? Is it safe to say that you are becoming confounded and disappointed about your condition? Have you been told to leave God and this Congregation thing? Have you been advised like Task to revile God and pass on? Either in light of the fact that your circumstance is falling apart constantly and your family, companions and well-wishers have abandoned you. Kindly, don't say in light of the fact that your recuperating has not come, that you will surrender. No, that isn't the desire of God for you. There is still expectation. For in Occupation 14:7 it is composed in this way, "For there is potential for a tree, in the event that it is chopped down, that it will grow in the future, and that its shoots will not cease."In Jeremiah 30:17 God said, "For I will reestablish wellbeing to you and mend your injury". What's more, in Jeremiah 31:17 the sacred writing likewise records that "there is potential for your future".

At the point when Peter was tied in with soaking in the water that would have annihilated him, he immediately recollected that Jesus was with him, and he yelled like visually impaired Bartimaeus as loud as possible and said, 'ace, save me' and he was in a split second conveyed. Do you recall that what made Peter to stroll on water was confidence? Do you additionally recollect that the issue which made Peter to sink into the water was that his confidence was gone after? I couldn't say whether your confidence is enduring an onslaught at the present time, by the specialists of dimness? Have you given up to Satan's assault on your confidence? Has the tension of your wellbeing status made you to leave your confidence in God, and you have gone to Egypt for help? In the event that you have neglected, may I rapidly advise you that in Hymn 16:4 the sacred text records that "the people who go to different divine beings, duplicate their difficulty". Has the condition of your wellbeing further developed even after you deserted your confidence in God? Assuming the test is still there, kindly don't kick the bucket in your misstep, just return to your producer and accommodate with Him, He will most likely retouch your wrecked life.

ACCOMMODATE WITH GOD.

The second job a debilitated individual necessities to play to get heavenly mending is the capacity to express no to sin and move toward God for pardoning and benevolence. It will be extremely off-base for one to be intentionally breaking the core of God, through insubordinate demonstrations of noncompliance but anticipate that He should answer one's request for mending. According to for this reason the sacred writing, "God excuses generally your injustice, and recuperates your infection" (Song 103:3). Do you believe God should recuperate you from that satanic bolt of contamination called affliction? Have you been imploring, and the response isn't impending, but your condition has not gotten to the next level? I think it is the ideal opportunity for you to move ground, separate your neglected ground of unconfessed sin, the time has come to genuinely look for God in compromise, until He comes to rain uprightness on you (Hosea 10:12).

In 2006 and 2007, I and some other splashed with somebody who was extremely debilitated and wouldn't admit his transgression and set things straight. However, since we were not God that knows it all, his evildoing was subsequently uncovered when it was late. Tragically, he passed on in that ailment. May you never pass on in that affliction? Also, may you always remember that accommodating with your creator is so fundamental, taking everything into account.

You Influence the world

WELCOME A CLERGYMAN

"Are those of you wiped out? They ought to require the older folks of the Congregation and have them supplicate over them, blessing them with oil for the sake of the Ruler. The request of confidence will save the debilitated, and the Master will raise them up; and anybody who has committed sin will be pardoned" (James 5:14-15).

The reality stays that there are a few difficult infections, which will go after an individual so severely, that such an individual will find it undeniably challenging to make and think for revolutionary petition of confidence to draw in the finger of God for divine recuperating. Also, God talking through St. James, taught that there is need for a wiped out individual to have their impact for getting their mending, by welcoming the elderly folks of the congregation (the priests), who will come and have their influence by serving recuperating to the debilitated patient. Also, in doing this, adored, due to the elevated degree of rot in this present reality, one ought to be exceptionally mindful so as not to welcome individuals that their heart isn't yet broken, having no compassion for yourself as well as your difficulties; rather, are just keen on material additions. No, don't welcome them, for these sorts of people are not blessed for that mission. "Furthermore, these signs will go with the people who accept, by utilizing my name they will project out evil presences; they will talk in new tongues; they will get snakes in their grasp, and on the off chance that they drink any dangerous thing, it won't hurt them; they will lay their hands on the wiped out, and they will recuperate" (Imprint 16:17-18).What assuming the priest you welcomed or went to, for help, turn you down or even called you canine like the experience of a specific lady that met Jesus with her kid. A few priests may not be harsh or strong enough to close you down, yet the long conventions might be the issue that will get you bothered or exhausted. In such conditions, you are supposed to practice persistence however on the off chance that you can hardly pause, then proceed to implore out, in light of the fact that the God you will meet in that service for wonder can likewise come to your home this second.

Accordingly, assuming you at any point fall debilitated and you have the solidarity to implore yourself out of that ailment, such as Lord Hezekiah did in the book of

You Influence the world

Isaiah 38:2-3, feel free to make it happen. Yet, assuming you are down, and diverted, to such an extent that you even uncertainty the requests that you petition God for yourself, putting forth attempts to welcome or meet with the pastors for petitions to heaven isn't awkward, on the grounds that it is likewise one more approach to having your influence no longer any of Satan's concern. I want to believe that you actually recollect that St. Peter was a recuperating priest, at this point when his mother by marriage was debilitated, Jesus was welcome to come and mend her? Regardless of how blessed you are, don't permit self and Satan to cheat and misdirect you by thinking, that since you are a recuperating priest, that you needn't bother with the assistance or help of another pastor at whatever point you are out of luck.

GAINING FROM THE SHUNAMITE LADY

> *"He said, at this season sooner or later, you will embrace a child. She answered, no my Master, o godly man; don't trick your worker. The lady imagined and bore a child at that season, sooner or later, as Elisha had pronounced to her. At the point when the kid was more established, he went out one day to his dad among the collectors. He grumbled to his dad, goodness, my head! My head! The dad shared with his worker, convey him to his mom. He conveyed him and carried him to his mom; the kid sat on her lap until early afternoon, and he kicked the bucket. She went up and laid him on the bed of the righteous man, shut the entryway on him, and left. Then she called to her better half, and said, send me one of the workers and one of the jackasses, so I may rapidly go to the righteous man and return once more" (2 Lords 4:16-22).*

Clearly, this lady was excessively revolutionary, I appreciate her. She never gave in to whimpering, in any event, when her better half flopped horribly to have his impact as a dad to their hotly anticipated wonder child; that Satan went after within the sight of his dad in the ranch. This lady was deserted with her debilitated kid in a single corner of that shrubbery all. The facts confirm that her significant other and his laborers were there, yet the inquiry is, would they say they were truly there for her? Might it be said that they were not more keen on the homestead work than the lady and her debilitated kid? Simply envision the indiscreet demeanor showed by this spouse and father. If really he was occupied that exact second his child was gone after in his presence in the primary occasion, for what reason did he not show up promptly he completed what he was doing, however imprudently permitted his significant other to bear their aggravation alone, conveying the youngster on her laps from morning till early afternoon lastly surrendered? Cherished, why I respect this lady and each and every individual who depicts her sort of righteousness is that when her better half neglected to satisfy his obligations, she disregarded that shortcoming, showed by her significant other, and never tried to battle him or move her animosity to their laborers, no, she essentially gazed upward and recollected the Lord of Elisha, who is the source and sustainer of the existence of her kid.

Cherished, whenever hard times arise in your wellbeing or in regions around you, I believe that you should pause for a minute to consider the methodology of the Shunamite lady during her misfortune. Off kilter, I realize that affliction and different difficulties of life can be so weighty to convey, yet one ought to gain from this righteous lady on the most proficient method to convey and deal with one's difficulties God's own specific manner. The way that you as of now have a wellbeing challenge doesn't imply that you won't survive and emerge from it. The weight and the injury of that affliction is really troublesome, I get it, yet I exhort that you request that the Essence of God help you, so you won't despise God and the priests, and that you won't manhandle your family and wellbeing laborers, due to your test. Censure that fiend, and decline to sing the tunes of cynicism, stay positive; and that Egyptian you see today around you, you will see them no more (Mass migration 14:13).

GAINING FROM LORD HEZEKIAH

I treasure the extreme confidence that Ruler Hezekiah had. It moved him to supplicate the manner in which he did and God immediately mediated. It was Prophet Isaiah who gave Ruler Hezekiah that message from the Master, a message that seemed like a capital punishment. Was the message about the flight of the lord misleading? The response is no! For neither the prophet, nor the message was bogus. They were both right and precise. Then, at that point, for what reason did God adjust His perspective towards the lord, somebody might inquire? The response is straightforward. Dearest, in the event that there is a man with extremist confidence to ask like Ruler Hezekiah, there is a Divine being in paradise to constantly hear and reply. In Jews 11:5, the sacred writing says that "It was confidence that kept Enoch from dying."So, assuming you and I have Hezekiah's real's sort, there is no amount of danger and provocation from Satan that will shake or move us. Maybe, you don't know, may I rapidly advise you, that each disorder that assaults you regardless of how little, should be seen and treated as an evil spirit which resembles a weed (an undesirable grass or plant, developing among wheat).

Immediately, having perused sacred writings on mending and once more, I have presumed that there is no spot in the sacred writing, that the confidence of individuals or the people who brought them for recuperating were not needed prior to mending occurred. So set your confidence in motion.

PETITION

My dad and my God, I genuinely thank you for the endowment of life today. Despite the fact that I am not areas of strength for excessively, I thank you since I know, that a living canine is superior to a dead lion. According to father, in Jews 11:5, your assertion, that it was confidence, that held Enoch back from passing on. Subsequently, for the sake of Jesus, I order, that I will not pass on from this ailment. I order for the sake of Jesus, that I will live and affirm your decency goodness! Ruler, in life in living color. For the sake of Jesus, and by the force of the Essence of God, I come against any power or powers, which are liable for the ailments that are torturing me currently by fire. Any special stepped area which was laid out, anyplace under paradise, getting penances, to obliterate my life troublesome, on the grounds that I am serving the living God, who is otherwise called the fourth man in the fire, the lion of the clan of Judah, the vanquisher of evil spirit and the winner of death. Let any special stepped area, where my name, picture and cash, may have been taken to, by any specialists of murkiness, for any devilish exercises and profound

mischievousness, burst into flames and keep on consuming voraciously, until I at last survive and recuperate, all my legacy in Jesus name So be it.

SECTION FOUR

DIVINE WELLBEING - YOUR REDEMPTIVE RIGHT

At the point when you arrive at the understanding of the way that heavenly wellbeing is one of your redemptive privileges, there isn't anything you won't do to get (in experience) what is yours. At some point back, I had a chance of addressing gathering of God's kin some place on a subject, "Safeguard your legacy", and during my concentrate in anticipation of that program, I considered the narrative of the man Naboth in 1 Lords 21:1-16, contemplating on how he safeguarded his legacy with his blood. The explanation he kicked the bucket safeguarding what he had, was from the comprehension that the said legacy was given to him (by his progenitors) to keep, appreciate, secure and handover to the future. When Lord Ahab constrained him to give his legacy at any expense, Naboth just shared with him, live always O Ruler, your highness if it's not too much trouble, save your silver and gold for the castle depository, this legacy isn't really for sell.

Pause for a minute to contemplate on what it cost Jesus to recover humankind, the put-downs, treacheries, disavowals, and the agonies He went through. There isn't anything one wouldn't do to remain solid. At the point when your mentor or game expert ask you during practice in an exercise center, to lie on the floor, keep your hands on the floor and lift up your legs and down for thirty back to back times constantly without rest. Try not to rebel, since even Jesus additionally perspired lavishly in the nursery of Gethsemane just to recover you. At the point when your bite the dust titian request that you relinquish your number one food and beverages to remain sound, comply and recollect that Jesus additionally abstained for a really long time and forty evenings (Mathew 4:2). At the point when your primary care physician educates that you ought to quit smoking and drinking your #1 beverages, simply comply and remember that even Jesus was denied water when He was extremely parched. Lastly, as God had proactively educated in His promise, that His kids should avoid sex and infidelity, comply and don't arrange it by any means, if you truly need to remain solid both genuinely, inwardly, monetarily and profoundly

You Influence the world

"Adored, I supplicate that all might work out positively for you and that you might be healthy, similarly as it is well with your spirit" (3John 2). In this part, lets venture momentarily to God's promise which says that "God made us for incorruption and made us in his picture to live everlastingly, yet through Satan's jealousy, demise entered the world, and the people who have a place with his organization experience it" (Shrewdness 2:23-24).

The principal thing you ought to note here, is that as a reclaimed offspring of God, you are a picked race, an illustrious brotherhood, a blessed country, God's own kin and consequently don't have a place with the organization of Satan. The sacred writing clear shows that man was made awesome and upright like his maker. However, through the jealousy of Satan man, was attracted into transgression of insubordination which made his otherworldly wall to be broken. However, with the approaching of Christ, that lost position and legacy was reestablished, to such an extent that in Ephesians 2:6-10, the sacred text records that "God raised us up with him and situated us with him in the great spots in Christ Jesus, so in the ages to come he could show the immense wealth of his elegance through benevolence towards us in Christ Jesus. For by beauty, we have been saved through confidence, and this isn't our doing; it is the endowment of God not the aftereffect of works, so nobody might gloat. For we are what he has made us, made in Christ Jesus for good works, which God arranged before hand to be our lifestyle."

Somebody might ask, for what reason do you say that heavenly wellbeing is a devotee's right? Indeed, on the off chance that you are an offspring of God, divine wellbeing is your right on the grounds that the idea of the elderly person in you that was bound in shortcoming has been really reawakened by the penance of Christ Jesus on the cross of Calvary. Dearest, I want to believe that you actually realize that you and I are made in the picture and resemblance of God our maker. I additionally trust that you have not failed to remember that God the Dad, God the Child and God the Essence of God lives in us? Furthermore, that He (God) in us is far more prominent than the one (Satan) in the entire world who approaches causing individuals with chronic sickness?

You Influence the world

Dearest, assuming you really accept that Christ Jesus lives in you, do you imagine that He will permit Satan to beset your wellbeing? You should know that in the event that Jesus didn't extra individuals He met profaning the sanctuary, He won't allow anything that will bring you medical affliction. In Mass migration 34:14, the sacred writing records that our God is a desirous God who endures no opponent. Who is an opponent? The word adversary can be characterized as a rival, endeavoring to go against and get what only one individual can have. Only god legitimately owns your life, and not Satan who is a cheat; attempting to have what isn't his, and reap from where he has not planted. You might ask, on the off chance that heavenly wellbeing is really my redemptive right, for what reason do I fall wiped out? The following are the reasons.

JUSTIFICATIONS FOR WHY A DEVOTEE CAN FALL WIPED OUT

1. **Sin:** What is sin? Sin is any hint of defiant demonstrations, against the adoration for God to man. Sin can likewise be characterized as the overstepping of otherworldly regulations. It separates our profound wall (the support of covering around us). It makes us defenseless against the catches of Satan. Whenever we commit sin and neglect to admit and emerge from it rapidly, we give Satan an open greeting or willful access over our life. Sin annihilates our insusceptibility and breakdowns our profound endurance. Do we have any idea about that the name Samson signifies "sun rise", and the name Delilah signifies "bring low"? The exact instant sun rise committed an expensive error of picking "bring low" as his nearby partner, that was the second the eyes of his predetermination were stopped out by his foes.

   > *"Then certain individuals came, bringing to him a deadened man, conveyed by four of them. What's more, when they couldn't carry him to Jesus as a result of the group, they eliminated the rooftop above him; and in the wake of having dug through it, they let down the mat on which the disabled lay. At the point when Jesus saw their*

confidence, he shared with the immobile, child your transgressions are pardoned" (Imprint 2:3-6).

The above sacred text gives a model where sin was an immediate reason for disorder in the existence of a man. Notwithstanding sin and its adverse consequences, the companions of this deadened individual, could not have possibly endured to the degree of eliminating the top of a structure looking for Jesus, the best healer, all things considered. When the disabled was at long last carried down to Jesus; through the rooftop, He was moved by their confidence and essentially shared with the wiped out man, child your wrongdoings are pardoned, get your mat and go. Try not to pay attention to the people who are distraught at me for pardoning your transgressions and recuperating your infections. Simply proceed to recall sin no more (accentuation mine).

2. **Working without resting:** The human body requires rest now and again to appropriately keep on working. God, the maker and leader of the universe, laid on the seventh day after the heavenly work of creation, appointing that there ought to be a day off. You should treat the need to rest from work in a serious way, to stay away from pressure prompted diseases. A portion of these sicknesses incorporate coronary illness, strain migraines, high glucose, stoutness, misery and so on. God laid on the seventh day, what is your day off?

3. **Lack of activity:** Exercise is an actual work that one does to remain sound and become more grounded. Be that as it may, I will talk about practice here in two folds, profound and actual activities. Sacred writing sets hence "For actual preparation is valuable, however otherworldly preparation is of worth in all things and all around, since it holds guarantee for the life to come" (1Timothy 4:8). Like St. Paul properly noted here, profound activity is of more significance than physical, in light of the fact that profound activity engages one to have discretion, which will among different advantages, assist the person with succeeding in actual activity. Expecting one chooses to concentrate on the book of scriptures, supplicate and venerate God for thirty minutes

to one hour in the early hours of his/her consistently in storeroom; and quick routinely. There is no question, that the individual's life will be ablaze profoundly, and when one's life is ablaze, consuming for God, regardless of the amount Satan and his representatives might want to hurt him/her through infection, they won't ever succeed, in light of the fact that he/she will be exceptionally inaccessible, distant and un-killable. Fire up. Fr. Ejike Mbaka once said in one of his messages that, "Assuming you say you can swim in water, might you at any point likewise swim in fire?" Presently, let me share with us here, one of the impacts of absence of profound activity. Inability to take part in otherworldly activity, will make one succumb in the possession of their foes. Presently, having seen that profound activity has colossal award to our wellbeing. Allow us likewise to investigate the advantages of the second part of activity which I noted above as actual activity. Actual activity has proactively been characterized above as any actual work that you truly do to remain solid and stay more grounded. What are the advantages of actual activity?

(i) Exercise controls your weight.

(ii) It improves rest and sleep.

(iii) It boots your energy

(iv) It improves your mood.

(v) It fights health conditions and diseases.

On the off chance that one neglects to work-out consistently, the impacts will be the converse of the above benefits. Hence, if you truly need to remain better and more grounded, you should get up and consume a few calories.

4. **Eating wrongly:** that's what dieticians instruct "we are what we eat." Assuming you feed your body by eating adjusted diet instead of garbage,

you will be sound and more grounded. In some cases when individuals fall debilitated, it isn't really in light of the fact that they are in a profound sense malnourished yet because of unfortunate sustenance and sustenance of the body. It is likewise workable for one to profoundly be all around took care of truly however ineffectively took care of.

5. **Inadequate rest:** Neglecting to routinely have great rest of no less than six to seven hours might have negative, unfriendly consequences for one' shealth.

6. **Spiritual fiendishness and evil exercises:** Certain individuals experience serious chronic sickness today, in light of the exercises of the underhanded. In Precepts 4:16-17, sacred writing records hence, "Evil individuals can't rest except if they misunderstand followed through with something. They lay there except if they have harmed somebody. Evil and viciousness are like food and drink to them." Quite a long time back, a specific young fellow was doing great in business and chose to set aside and put away some cash for sometime later. Tragically for him, the older man to whom he endowed his speculation was naughty. At the point when he found that the young fellow' sin garment was valuing in esteem, he welcomed him for a beverage and harmed him, leaving him with a serious disorder which prompted his troublesome passing.

PETITION

Much obliged to you father, for the effortlessness, astuteness, information and comprehension of the reality, that heavenly wellbeing is my redemptive right. For the sake of Jesus Christ, and by the force of the Essence of God, I get elegance, to watch what I eat and drink, both actually and profoundly, to remain sound. For the sake of Jesus Christ, and by the force of the Essence of God, I get effortlessness, to give names decidedly and appropriately, to anything that comes my direction in Jesus name So be it. For the sake of Jesus, and by the force of the Essence of God, I get

effortlessness, to pick Authentic and right partners, that will not at all, cause me otherworldly shortcoming, mental and close to home injury, mental and conjugal emergencies, profession and professional mishap, or any sort of hindered in Jesus powerful name So be it.

SECTION FIVE

DIVINE MENDING IS OUR REDEMPTIVE RIGHT

Martin Luther Lord (Jr.) once expressed "Nothing on the planet is more hazardous than earnest obliviousness and reliable idiocy". What one doesn't have the foggiest idea, as a rule forecasts an impediment. In Hosea 4:6, the sacred text records subsequently, "My kin die for absence of information". The exact second we find that heavenly recuperating is our redemptive right; and we live genuinely accepting something very similar, affliction will have no territory over us. An extraordinary level of God's kin, get confounded each time we let them know that disorder is a wicked burden, and hence, isn't essential for what they ought to bear in being great devotees of Christ Jesus.

Indeed, I realize that our Master Jesus endured, and saved us through misery. However, the inquiry we ought to pose to ourselves sort of enduring did Jesus genuinely endure? Was it not disloyalty, refusal, affront, and mistreatment for taking every necessary step of His dad? At any point do we peruse in the Book of scriptures, that Jesus was conceded in the emergency clinic or that He needed to head off to some place to teach or favor individuals, and He was unable to go in light of the fact that He was extremely debilitated? Indeed, it is 100% right that enduring is essential for life, yet it is critical to comprehend what sort of anguish. For example, when a lady is at the place of conveyance, she normally goes through compressions, an interaction which accompanies serious torment. Moreso, when one is participated in hard, difficult work as an approach to procuring one's occupation, or for the promotion of God's realm, these are a sort of experiencing that one can acknowledge with satisfaction and nobility, and not the Evil bolt of need, sin and disorders.

Cherished, the principal thing I need to impart to us, in this section is that I have outright and all out faith in divine recuperating. My purposes behind this energetic conviction and confidence in divine recuperating is that I have seen various cases, where a few people were told by clinical faculty; that their wellbeing challenges have no clinical arrangement or cure, and when they went to God, they were supernaturally mended. One of the people I saw his case, even went to the emergency clinic in Germany looking for mending from clinical science, yet nothing occurred until God ventured into the case. My daringness, to accept and educate with energy regarding the matter of heavenly mending, is additionally roused by God's promise in Beginning 1:31which says that "God saw all that He had made, and to be sure, it was awesome".

Affliction is unwholesome, exceptionally awful thus hurtful, hence, was not among the beneficial things which God made and considered to be awesome. In the event that you have not been debilitated or cared for somebody who was truly wiped out, you won't comprehend me when I say that disorder is terrible. Thirdly, Jesus told a Gentile lady of Syrophoenician beginning, who came to Him with her little girl looking for redemption and recuperating (Imprint 7:27) "Let the kids be taken care of first, for it is just a tad ridiculous to take the youngsters' food and toss it to the canines." Metaphorically, Jesus insistently let the lady know that "Mending is the youngsters' bread." Subsequently, any man or lady, who is as of now washed by the blood of the sheep, is completely able to get recuperating from God since He is our dad and we are His youngsters. Dear peruser, don't permit Satan and his representatives to threaten you, recuperating is our redemptive right, since Yahweh Rapha, the best healer of any age is our dad. He is the rose of Sharon and the lily of the valley.

As an organic dad of four great kids, I and my exquisite spouse work constantly to guarantee that our youngsters feed well and don't get starved. I genuinely want to believe that you actually realize that it is the obligation of each and every parent to take care of their kids. Any kid who is loyal to its folks, need not ask for nourishment for days or years, prior to being taken care of? May I additionally help you that one to remember the fundamental necessities of person is food. Presently, let us reason together. Jesus let the lady know that carried her little girl to Him for redemption and recuperating that 'mending is the kids' bread.' I don't have any idea who is perusing this book at the present time, yet as a dad, I can guarantee you out of involvement that bread is the least demanding and most normal food that youngsters can get.

You Influence the world

Accordingly, assuming Jesus let the lady know that recuperating is the kids' bread, my comprehension here is that.

1. Healing is the unquestionable right of each and every offspring of God: Would you say you are an offspring of God? Furthermore, you are debilitated by and by; proceed to search for your right. The opportunity has arrived; you, I mean you that is perusing this book at the present time! You have grown up. You are not a slave. Along these lines, quit living like one, and piously ponder profoundly, at what St. Paul composed here, "Presently what I mean [when I discuss youngsters and their guardians] is this: the length of the main beneficiary is a kid, he doesn't contrast by any means from a slave despite the fact that he is the [future proprietor and] expert of all [the estate]; however he is under [the authority of [guardians and family overseers or directors until the date set by his dad [when he is of age]."

2. Healing is so natural to get when you know it's your right: "Ask, and you will get; look for, and you will find; thump, and the entryway will be opened to you. For each and every individual who asks, gets, and anybody who looks for, finds, and the entryway will be opened to the people who thump. Could any of you who are fathers give your child a stone when he requests bread? Or on the other hand could you give him a snake when he requests a fish? However awful as you may be, you know how to give beneficial things to your kids. The amount more, then, will your dad in paradise give beneficial things to the people who ask him!" (Mathew 7:7-11).

3. Divine mending is completely paid for; consequently, you and I are to get it uninhibitedly without charge of any sort: In Isaiah 52:3 it is expressed, "The Sovereign Master tells His kin, when you became slaves, no cash was paid for you; similarly nothing will be paid to liberate you". So be savvy to the point of taking off from any individual, who is requesting that you pay the person in question cash since the person in question needs to appeal to God for you. It is not necessarily

the case that you can't see the value in the pastors who supplicate with you during your snapshots of emergencies in the event that you can bear the cost of it without stress. An entertaining story was recounted the way that a specific man said he planned to supplicate a specific family out of the soul of destitution. It is amusing on the grounds that, that deceiver, requested that they give him 100,000 naira. In 1Corinthians 14:20 KJV, the Sacred text says, "In understanding, be men". In this way, in the event that you are presently not a child, don't permit yourself to be bamboozled by individuals who ought to gain from you.

4. Healing happens or happens quicker when our life is perfect: "See, the Ruler's hand isn't too short to even consider saving, nor his ear too dull to even think about hearing. Rather, our injustices have been obstructions among us and our God, and our wrongdoings have concealed his face from us so he doesn't hear. For our hands are debased with blood, and our fingers with wrongdoing; your lips have spoken lies, our tongue murmurs mischievousness" (Isaiah 59:1-3). Satan is a backstabber, he is the person who deludes individuals to defy God and live in transgression; and when one turns into a routine miscreant, it won't be well before a particularly individual's life will be dirtied and put crooked in a profound sense. However, through the assistance of the Essence of God, at whatever point such individual leaves their life of transgression and gets back to God for leniency, all aspects of their life, officially disengaged by wrongdoing will rapidly be fixed by the Lord of affection and kindness who says in (Romans 9: 16) "So it depends not on human will or effort, but rather on God who has pity".

Divine force of kindness and empathy,
Look with feel sorry for upon me.
Father, let me call you Father,
Tis thy kid gets back to you.

You Influence the world

Melody

Jesus Master, I request leniency,
Let me not entreat to no end.
Every one of my transgressions I presently loathe them,
At no point ever will I sin in the future.

Refrain 2

By my wrongdoings I have merited,
Demise and unending hopelessness.
Damnation with every one of its agonies and tortures,
What's more, forever.

Refrain 3

By my transgressions I have deserted,
Right and guarantee to paradise above.
Where the holy people cheer until the end of time,
In an unlimited ocean of adoration.

Refrain 4

See our Guardian angel, dying, biting the dust,
On the Cross of Calvary.
To that Cross my transgressions have nailed him,
However he drains and kicks the bucket for me (CHB Song 194)

Petition

God the dad, God the Child and God the Essence of God, I thank you for all you have accomplished for me before, what you are doing at present, and what you are going to do. I likewise need to thank you, on the grounds that, as a genuine offspring of the realm, I know and accept, that every one of the endowments, which are intended for the children and little girls of the realm, likewise have a place with me. In this way, for the sake of Jesus Christ of Nazareth, I order each soul of disorder and sicknesses, to leave me at the present time. Through the weapon of the blood of Jesus, and by the discharge of the Essence of God, I discharge myself from each hint of shortcoming and sicknesses. I order that I (notice your name) have a place with God and Him alone. Furthermore, in light of the fact that my body is the sanctuary of the Essence of God, I invite Him, to totally assume control over my life at this moment. I accept my mending right now in Jesus name So be it.

SECTION SIX

SATAN IS THE CREATOR OF INFECTION

Cherished, never whenever acknowledge ailment of any sort in your life as the desire of God, since when you do, you are perpetually saying that the satanic bolts took shots at you from the pit of misery, is God's will, which isn't and won't ever be. Offspring of God, in the event that you at any point tragically acknowledge disorder as the desire of God as opposed to dismissing and reprimanding it, you might be everlastingly distressed, mistreated, scared, controlled, and toward the end, neediness and passing will be unavoidable. At the point when you start to encounter these, your tunes and declarations all the time will be one of agonies, distresses and hardships.

Many individuals don't have any idea (perhaps on account of obliviousness) that Satan is (straightforwardly or in a roundabout way) the reason for all disorders. However, hardly any things were clarified in sacred writing. For example, on account of Work, we are informed that Satan was straightforwardly liable for putting the bubbles (affliction) on him.

> *"Thus, Satan went out from the presence of the Master, and incurred detestable wounds for Occupation from the bottom of his foot to the crown of his head"* (Job 2:7).

At the point when Paul spoke about his most memorable lesson to the Gentiles, he announced that infection was brought about by the persecution of Satan, and that our Master Jesus was made manifest; to annihilate without kindness every one of crafted by the devil."The child of God was uncovered for this reason, to obliterate crafted by Satan" (1 John 3:8).

> *How God blessed Jesus of Nazareth with Essence of God and with power; how he approached accomplishing something beneficial and recuperating all who were persecuted by Satan, for God was with Him* (Acts 10:38).

Our Ruler Jesus Himself credited to Satan; the hardship of the one who had been headed for a very long time in the good news of Luke.

You Influence the world

> "He was showing in one of the places of worship on the day off. View, there was a lady who had a feeling of sickness eighteen years. She was twisted around and could not the slightest bit fix herself up. At the point when Jesus saw her, he called her, and shared with her, 'lady, you are liberated from your ailment." He laid hands on her, and quickly she stood upright and celebrated God. The leader of the temple, being resentful on the grounds that Jesus had recuperated on the time of rest, shared with the large number, "There are six days in what men should work. Thusly, come on those days and be mended, and not on the day off!" Consequently, the Master responded to him, "You scoundrel! Doesn't every last one of you free his bull or his jackass from the slow down on the time of rest, and lead him away to water?" Should not this lady, being a girl of Abraham, whom Satan had bound eighteen long years, be liberated from this servitude on the day off?" (Luke 13:10-16).

Dearest, we plainly see from the sacred writing over that insidious spirits are the reason for some burdens? On account of this lady, who is likewise a little girl of Abraham, it was the soul of illness that distorted her for quite some time. Be that as it may, when the malicious soul was projected out of her, by Jesus, who is the top, everything being equal, she was liberated and in a split second recovered her ordinary height.

Satan is the creator of ailment and torment; he is the one releasing dread on people of kindness. The comprehension of this reality is the very reason you see individuals of God wherever petitioning God for the wiped out individuals time without number. The Congregation even takes this battle against Satan, past the otherworldly to the physical; by building emergency clinics and preparing her priests, as clinical specialists in their consistent battle against Satan, who generally tries to burden individuals with transgression and ailments.

> *"Be level-headed [well adjusted and self-disciplined], be dependably ready and mindful. That foe of yours, Satan, slinks around like a thundering lion [fiercely hungry], looking for somebody to eat up"* (1 Peter 5:8).

You Influence the world

I will impart to you, four significant things that were divulged in the above sacred text, that we shouldn't fail to remember in a rush.

FOUR THINGS YOU OUGHT TO BE FAMILIAR WITH SATAN AS OUR ADVERSARY.

1. The fiend (in his mission to eat up) is conscious, giving his best, hence, devotees should constantly be ready and mindful: God talking through Prophet Isaiah taught, that devotees as an issue of earnestness ought to alarm say "Alert, conscious, put on your delightful pieces of clothing, Goodness! Jerusalem, the sacred city; for the uncircumcised and the messy will as of now not come into you. Shake yourself from the residue, emerge, o hostage Jerusalem; free yourself of chains around your neck, o hostage girl of Zion. For the Ruler says this, you were sold in vain, and you will be reclaimed, however not with cash" (Isaiah 52:1-3). Your powerlessness to acknowledge the appeal of God, through His Prophets to remain conscious, will draw in Satan into your homestead, planting unafraid at all he wants.

2. The fiend is our adversary: Here, St. Peter decidedly called Satan our adversary; thus, he isn't our companion and won't ever be. Regardless of how he camouflages himself, professing to help us, he is a liar and just searches for a valuable chance to obliterate. I want to believe that we obviously see that St. Peter never said that our neighbor, partner, mother or father by marriage in the town is our foe. He never did, he essentially said that our foe is Satan. Does it imply that Satan can't utilize someone to go after us? He can. So whenever he does, rather than drawing in the vessel (man and so on) that Satan uses to go after us, it is significant we utilize our profound weapon against Satan and not the vessel, "Our wrestle isn't against flesh [contending just with physical opponents], yet against the rulers, against the powers, against the world powers of this [present] obscurity, against the otherworldly powers of evil in the glorious [supernatural] places" (Ephesians 6:12).

You Influence the world

3. The fiend sneaks around like a thundering lion: Satan just lurks like a lion, he isn't one and can never be one. Have you at any point considered the reason why Satan ordinarily prefers to work in obscurity? The response is straightforward, he fears the Light, which is Jesus in us the desire for greatness. In Matthew 13:25, Jesus told a story, on how a man established wheat in his ranch, and keeping in mind that everybody was snoozing, a foe proceeded to establish weed in the homestead. Have we at any point asked ourselves, in the event that Satan is really strong as he guarantees, for what reason did he not plant the detestable weed while everybody was alert?

4. The fiend is furiously eager, looking for somebody to eat up: As indicated by Longman Word reference of contemporary English, the word gobble up, essentially means to eat up with covetousness, to consume insatiably, to take advantage of, to obliterate, to gobble up, to go through, to squander, to destroy, etc. All in all, assuming I figure out that I have an adversary, who is savagely ravenous, looking to do to me all that are recorded above, how then will I respond, to beat this rival? The response is exceptionally basic and available. According to in James 4:7-8, sacred text, "So submit to [the authority of] God. Oppose Satan [stand firm against him] and he will escape from you. Come near God [with a humble heart] and He will come near you. Clean up, you heathens; and filter your [unfaithful] hearts, you twofold disapproved [people]." It is extremely perilous for you to draw in Satan into a fight, when you realize that you are exceptionally distant from God; either in light of a specific evil propensity, which you have not yet admitted or apologized from, and dread. For the wellbeing of Christ, for what reason should a devotee be reluctant to oppose Satan, when the person has been washed by the valuable blood of the sheep? Regardless of whether we like it, in the event that we don't submit to God, we can't avoid Satan, and on the off chance that we don't avoid him, he won't ever escape from wrecking us. In Ephesians 2:6, 1:20-22, God uncovered to us that as adherents, we are not in a similar class with

Satan. We are situated with Christ far above territories and powers. May the Ruler reprimand you Satan! Say this request with me.

Petition

For the sake of Jesus Christ, and by the force of the Essence of God, I thank you father, for bringing me into your presence this second. My Ruler and my God, I ask you lenient dad, to pardon every one of my transgressions, and wash me clean, from every one of my wrongdoings in Jesus name So be it. For the sake of Jesus Christ, I reject Satan, and all his vacant commitments, duplicity, mistreatment, control, fixation, contamination, postponement, disavowal and command over my life, So be it. For the sake of Jesus Christ, and by the force of the Essence of God, I submit to God my producer, and I oppose any devil that is answerable for all hardships, dread, need, tension, backwardness, postponement and unfruitfulness, and I order them out of my life right presently by fire in Jesus name, So be it. [Say "I cover myself with the blood of Jesus Christ" seven times].

SECTION SEVEN

THE MOST EFFECTIVE METHOD TO SUPPORT YOUR RECUPERATING

In this section, I will divulge a few essential jobs that you really want to play to remain or stay recuperated after a mending wonder has occurred in your life, on the grounds that an extraordinary number of God's kin who accept their healings either in meetings or campaigns, later lose it in light of a portion of the things we will find in this part. Along these lines, it is one thing to accept your recuperating and one more to remain mended.

God is the source and sustainer of mending. In this way, to think about one's recuperating being supported without God is unimaginable. In John 21:3, the day the missionaries went fishing as opposed to remaining, centering and doing what they were blessed and delegated to do, unbelievable disappointment ventured into their lives, since God isn't focused on what He didn't commission. He doesn't support what He didn't begin. He isn't committed to complete what He didn't creator.

For example, any day that Satan goes after your wellbeing, the primary thing you ought to do is to approach God and not to rush or submit yourself to the hands of a clinical staff, who might wind up exploring different avenues regarding your life, and when it is past the point of no return, you will then make sure to call God. I believe you should take note of, that this isn't ın no method for sabotaging the spot of wellbeing laborers. My point here is to include God first, before each and every other choice or move you might make concerning your recuperating. God is the source and sustainer of recuperating. I truly want to believe that you might have heard the clinical faculty offer expressions like, "we treat, however God recuperates." Presently assuming the clinical staff additionally perceive the way that Yahweh Rapha alone is the healer, and you approach Him, sound judgment ought to help you what to do.

You Influence the world

SIX REASONS, WHY INDIVIDUALS LOSE THEIR MENDING

1. Wrong insights/conviction: Numerous Christians, who look for recuperating from God, imagine that each mending should be moment or what we call mending wonders. These individuals tragically work themselves out of their recuperating by their fretfulness and what they say. "Demise and life are in the force of the tongue" (Saying 18:21). We should note in this way, that only one out of every odd recuperating will be moment. A few healings take a continuous cycle to be completely idealized (see Imprint 8:22-25). I ask you, not to disavow your recuperating, through off-base discernment, reckless and negative expressions.

2. Wrong conviction and not knowing the blessing of a Prophet: "Elisha sent a courier to him, saying, 'Go, wash in the Jordan multiple times, and your tissue will be reestablished, and you will be spotless. 'Yet, Naaman ended up being furious and disappeared, saying, 'I felt that for me he would have without a doubt emerged, and stand approach the name of the Master his God, and would wave his hands over the spot, and fix the uncleanliness!" (2Kings 5:10-11). In light of the exercises of certain specialists of dimness who call themselves Prophets yet are somewhat scalawags, many find it extremely challenging to trust God in His prophets while looking for mending. Envision the show between the Prophet Elisha and Naaman. Today is exceptionally thoughtful that even, certain individuals needing mending actually go to God through His Prophets, with a similar demeanor and mindset of Naaman.

3. It is extremely off-base for you to coordinate a priest of God on the most proficient method to pastor to you during a segment of petition to control mending. All things considered, the priest is blessed, delegated and situated to get from God and afterward impart paradise's brain to you, and not the alternate way round. "They rose promptly toward the beginning of the day and went out into wild of Tekoa. As they went out, Jehoshaphat stood and expressed, "Pay attention to me, Judah, and you

occupant of Jerusalem! Have faith in Yahweh your God, so you will be laid out! Trust his Prophets, so you will thrive" (2Chronicles 20:20). Somebody once said that "in your Prophet is your benefit",

4. I thusly prompt you not to deprecate the Prophets appointed by God, the sacred text says, "By a Prophet Yahweh brought Israel up out of Egypt, and by a Prophet he was protected" (Hosea 12:13). That's what reality stays, despite the fact that a few self-acclaimed Prophets, who have their eyes fixed exclusively on material things, are caught up with deluding and confounding individuals through phony and debased forecasts; God actually has endless people, who are genuinely dedicated in their service as Prophets today.

5. Transfer of moral obligation: Certain individuals lose their recuperating on the grounds that they believe God and others should accomplish for them, how they ought to help themselves. This disposition can likewise be viewed as designation of obligation and causes individuals to lose their mending. In 1 Corinthians 3:6, we see an ideal illustration of division of work. In this sacred writing, the obligation of St. Paul was planting; the obligation of Apollos was watering, while God Himself was liable for the development of what was planted and watered. Regardless of how well disposed you are with a clinical specialist, he can endorse prescriptions for you; he can't take it for your sake. In Imprint 9:23 Jesus shared with the dad of the debilitated kid "It's anything but a question of what I can do, yet it involves what you can accept." Darling, there are two things that God can never accomplish for us, regardless of how long we may yearn for them.

   i. What has been finished.

   ii. What He advised us to do.

"While heading to Jerusalem Jesus was going through the locale among Samaria and Galilee. As he entered a town, ten pariahs moved toward him. Staying away, they called out, saying, Jesus, Expert, show kindness toward us!

You Influence the world

> *At the point when he saw them, he shared with them, 'Proceed to show yourselves to the ministers.' And as they went, they were made clean"* (Luke 17:11-14).

The ten men in the above sacred writing, that were genuinely burdened with the soul of uncleanliness, requested that the Expert mediate in their disaster, and Jesus in a split second answered by giving them a guidance, on what they ought to do. They did precisely exact thing they were told to do and accepted their recuperating. The expert's part towards their recuperating was to give a guidance, while theirs was to comply and do the request. Jesus didn't follow them to the ministers, they needed to comply with guidance they were given. On the off chance that these outcasts were a few people of today, they might have contended with Jesus saying, would you say you are not mindful that the law of our property limits us as outsiders from relating with others?

Companions, may I rapidly advise you, that if you would rather not lose your mending, at times nature and a few conventions should be pardoned. Indeed, even a few difficult side effects should be disregarded, by perpetual and revolutionary statement who can be depended on, over your wellbeing and healings. Assuming the untouchables were alright with their wiped out state, and never tried to emerge from their restrictions, Satan would have threatened them for eternity.

1. Abandoning the word which is God's remedies for wellbeing and healings: As indicated by Adages 4:20-22, the expression of God is restorative and hence, has the ability to mend and support anybody that gives sufficient consideration to it. The essayist of the letter to the Jews in Jews 4:12 lets us know that God's statement is dynamic and alive; it is more keen than every one of the blades and needle that is accessible in the best clinic in the entire world set up. God's assertion infiltrates all over the place and consequently, has the ability to win, divulge and recognize what the clinical science has no answer for. I couldn't say

whether you have at any point had an encounter where somebody who was exceptionally wiped out, went to the emergency clinic for examination, and after series of tests and conclusions was informed that by their discoveries, the person in question isn't debilitated in any way, yet the individual is biting the dust? One sibling Amos was told by his PCP, that the main answer for his chronic sickness was careful activity, and when he rose up to leave the specialist's office after the interview; a similar specialist who is a Muslim, got back to him and shared with him, are you a Christian? Proceed to supplicate, And to the greatness of His name, when the matter was accounted for to the Christian people group, they asked and infused the radiance of integrity into Amos' life, and he was restored, without going through a medical procedure of any sort. In Beginning sections one and two we obviously see that God's assertion has imaginative capacity.

2. Doubt: Uncertainty is absence of certainty and trust that God is willing and fit for doing at all; He said He will do. Question is a perilous weapon which Satan uses to hold the uninformed bound and ceaselessly deny them their privileges or endowments from God. Notwithstanding the kindness of God, shown Naaman, through his worker clarifying the prophet's guidance for him and assisting him with building confidence, Naaman would have stayed an outsider his whole life. In 2Kings 5:13, "his worker went dependent upon him and said, sir, in the event that the prophet had advised you to accomplish something troublesome, you would have gotten it done. Presently for what reason mightn't you at any point wash yourself, as he said, and be relieved"? As a matter of fact, question is a dangerous infection, it permits you to peruse the sacred texts on recuperating, pay attention to the motivated messages on mending wonders, however purges you of the solidarity to follow up on the 'Word' you read, or 'the message' you paid attention to, that would have set you ablaze of freedom until the end of time.

Cherished the time has come to dispense with your uncertainty, and genuinely trust the expression of God, and pursue choice to follow up on them drastically. Could it be said that you are in a difficult situation? Check this sacred text out,

"God is our shelter and strength [mighty and impenetrable], an exceptionally present and very much demonstrated help in a difficult situation. Consequently, we won't fear, however the earth ought to change and however the mountains be shaken and slip into the core of the ocean, however its waters thunder and froth, however the mountains shudder at its thundering. There is a waterway whose streams make happy the city of God, the blessed residence of the most high" (Hymn 46:1-4).

3. Fear: What is dread? Dread is verification that you don't have the foggiest idea how powerful your creator is, and His capacity to safeguard you consistently. What is dread? Dread is misleading, and bogus is whatever isn't accurate. Dread is that evil weapon, which makes you see yourself as a disappointment, making you think or accept that you can't make it. Anything that makes you to consider or envision a mountain out of mole slope is called dread. Dread is communicated in dialects with the way things are as of now past the point of no return, I can't make it, I won't succeed, I can't rest isolated, I will upchuck on the off chance that I eat it, etc. Do you have any idea that the deadened man that Jesus requested to get his mat and go in Imprint 2:11 was exceptionally wiped out and can't help himself? Do you additionally recollect that it was his companions that carried him to Jesus for mending through the top of the structure, at this point when he heard Jesus tell him pick your mat and go; he did, and never expected that he could fall assuming he endeavored to make it happen? Might it at any point be that your absence of intensity to have your influence out of that constraint right currently is on the grounds that you are apprehensive? In the event that God says you ought to fear not, it is vital to comply and fear not, to make the commitment of God (e.g., mending) your experience.

You Influence the world

USEFUL WAYS OF SUPPORTING MENDING.

You should stay associated with God (the healer) by:

[a] Engaging in concentrated and unending supplication. In Song 91:1, the sacred text records that "He who stays in the mystery spot of the most high will stay steady and fixed under the shadow of the all-powerful [whose power no adversary can withstand]".

[b] Engage in extremist applause and love of confidence: Indeed, you must be earnest and revolutionary enough in your acclaim and love to God. Guarantee that the main time you participate in applause and love to God isn't when everything around you is functioning admirably. Dedicate your opportunity to love Him in all conditions, regardless of whether the weather conditions is great. In Acts 16:23-25 it is stated, "In the wake of striking them ordinarily [with the rods], they tossed them into jail, ordering the corrections officer to safely monitor them. He, having gotten such a [strict] order, tossed them into the internal jail [dungeon] and secured their feet in the stocks [in a horrifying position]. However, about 12 PM when Paul and Silas were imploring and singing psalms of recognition to God, and the detainees were paying attention to them; unexpectedly there was an incredible quake, so [powerful] that the actual underpinnings of the jail were shaken and on the double every one of the entryways were opened and everybody's chains were loosened".

[c] Eating the bread of life [Which is the expression of God and the Heavenly Eucharist or communion]: When you quit eating your typical dinner consistently, your wellbeing will be impacted, notice that deficiency of craving some of the time is the side effect of ailment. In John 6:35 "Jesus answered to them, I'm the bread of life. The person who comes to me won't ever be ravenous, and the person who has faith in me [as saviour] won't ever be parched [for that one will be supported spiritually]. Would you like to stay sound, after your mending has been supernaturally gotten? Feel free to eat the bread of life. Likewise, in John 6:53-56, Jesus proceeded with His educating, and told them, "I

guarantee you most seriously, except if you eat the tissue of the Child of man drink His blood, you won't have life in yourselves. The person who eats My tissue and beverages My blood has everlasting life, and I will raise him up on the last day. For My tissue is genuine food, and My blood is genuine beverage. He who eats My tissue and beverages My blood stays in Me, and I in him".

2. You should ensure, that your profound wall is very much strengthened, since, supposing that you permit it to be indiscreetly broken, your foe will involve it as an entrance to assault and attack you freely (Mathew 12:43-45).
3. You should acknowledge the honorable reality, more than the sensations of your body: In 2 Corinthians 5:7, it is expressed, "For we live with conviction, by focusing on the subtle". Sentiments are the voice of the tissue. Assuming you stroll by sentiments, you are being overwhelmed by the tissue. You can't stroll by sentiments and be an effective Christian. Recollect that the things you give admittance to your life, will either free or keep you in servitude (Romans 4:18-20). Besides, any tree that isn't taller than you can never give you a shade.
4. You should practice your confidence continually, for power isn't dynamic, until confidence is worked out: In Acts 10:38, the Book of scriptures says, that Jesus was blessed by the Sacred Apparition and power and that He approached accomplishing something useful; and at some point, as He was en route to Jairus' home, many swarmed Him. However, the main individual that truly partaken in the totality of His power that day, was a lady with the issue of blood, who fundamentally practiced her confidence (Imprint 5:25-29). Really, power isn't dynamic, except if confidence is worked out. Hence, assuming you truly need the recuperating you get to be maintained, feel free to set your confidence in motion.
5. You should keep your ears open to day to day knowing about the blessed messages: Thusly, your confidence will be lifted enormously; and when your confidence is lifted, you will be moved or roused to do

what appears to be humanly unthinkable, (Mathew 14:25-29). One of my tutors had a stomach ulcer that truly managed him. It kept him from fasting works out. However, one specific day, he experienced the force of integrity and his confidence rose, he closed inside him, nothing more will be tolerated and that the evil torment brought ulcer had over remained it's gladly received and accordingly should leave his body. He roughly concluded to accomplish something that a ulcer patient shouldn't do. He was roused by the expression of God which he heard, fortified by the Essence of God and abstained from food and water from 6am to 6pm and to the brilliance of God, that bolt of affliction was forever removed from his body.

6. Concentrate on mending sacred texts and retain them: "My child, focus on my words and learn; open your ears to my truisms. Try not to allow them to escape from your sight; keep them in the focal point of your heart. For they are life; to the people who track down them, and mending and wellbeing to all their tissue" (Adages 4:20-22).

HERE ARE A PORTION OF THE RECUPERATING SACRED WRITINGS THAT WILL HELP YOU

A. "He said, assuming you will tenaciously pay attention to Yahweh your God's voice, and will do what is squarely in his eyes, and will focus on his rules, and keep every one of his sculptures, I will put none of the sicknesses on you, which I have placed on the Egyptians; for I'm Yahweh who recuperates you" Departure 15:26

B. "Then they cry to Yahweh in their difficulty, he saves them out of their upsets. He sends his assertion, and recuperates them, and conveys them from their grave (Song 107:19-20).

C. "He told her, girl, your confidence has made you well. Go in harmony and be relieved of your illness" (Imprint 5:34).

D. "All the hoards looked to contact Him, for power emerged from Him and mended them all" (Luke 6:19).

You Influence the world

E. "Is any of you wiped out? Allow him to require the seniors of the gathering, and allow them to ask over him, blessing him with oil for the sake of the Master, and the request of confidence will recuperate him who is debilitated, and the Ruler will raise him up. On the off chance that he carried out sins, he will be excused" (James 5:14-15).

F. "He himself bore our wrongdoings in his body on the tree, that we, having kicked the bucket to sins, could live to nobility. You were recuperated by his injuries" (1 Peter 2:24).

G. "Now the Ruler is the Soul and where the Soul of the Master is, there is freedom" (2 Corinthians 3:17).

H. "He recuperates the split in heart and predicament up their injuries" (Hymn 147:3).

I. "Yahweh will detract from you all disorder; and he will put none of the underhanded infections of Egypt, which you know, on you, however will lay them on every one of the people who can't stand you" (Deuteronomy 7:15).

J. "Jesus went about in all Galilee, showing in their gathering places, teaching the Goodnews of the realm, and mending each illness and each affliction among individuals" (Mathew 4:23).

K. "After these things, Jesus disappeared to the opposite side of the Ocean of Galilee, which is additionally called the ocean of Tiberias. An incredible huge number followed him, since they saw his signs which he did on the individuals who were debilitated" (John 6:1-2).

L. "Beloved, I supplicate that you might thrive no matter what and be solid, even as your spirit succeeds" (3 John 1:2).

M. "Behold, I will bring it wellbeing and fix, and I will fix them; and I will uncover to them overflow of harmony and truth" (Jeremiah 33:6).

You Influence the world

N. "Heal me, O Yahweh, and I will be recuperated. Save me, and I will be saved; for you are my acclaim" (Jeremiah 17:14).

O. "For I will reestablish wellbeing to you, and I will recuperate you of your injuries, says Yahweh; since they have called you an untouchable, saying, it is Zion whom no man pursues" (Jeremiah 30:17).

P. "He won't fear detestable news. His heart is immovable, confiding in Yahweh" (Song 112:7).

Q. "Then your light will break out as the morning, and your recuperating will show up rapidly; then your nobility will go before you, and Yahweh's greatness will be your back monitor" (Isaiah 58:8).

R. "You will serve Yahweh your God, and He will favor your bread and your water, and I will remove disorder from among you" (Departure 23:25).

S. "Oh Ruler my God, I cried to you for help, and you have recuperated me" (Song 30:2).

T. "But he was penetrated for our offenses. He was squashed for our evildoings. The discipline that brought our tranquility was on him; and by his injuries we are mended" (Isaiah 53:5).

U. "If we admit our wrongdoings, he is steadfast and equitable to excuse us the transgressions, and to purge us from all indecency" (1 John 1:9).

V. "That it very well may be satisfied which was spoken through Isaiah the prophet, saying, he took our ailments, and bore our illnesses" (Mathew 8:17).

W. "I call paradise and earth to observer against you today that I have set before your life and passing, the gift and the revile. Thusly, pick life, that you might live, you and your relatives" (Deuteronomy 30:19). Your will to live can support you when you are wiped out, yet if lose it, your last expectation is no more" (Adages 18:14).

X. "But if the Soul of him who raised up Jesus from the dead abides in you, he who raised up Christ Jesus from the dead will likewise give life to your human bodies through his Soul who stays in you" (Romans 8:11).

Y. "If my kin, who are called out to by me, will lower themselves, supplicate, look for my face, and abandon their fiendish behavior; then I will hear from paradise, will pardon their transgression, and will recuperate their territory" (2 Annals 7:14).

Z. "And He will clear away every remove from their eyes; and there will be no more demise; there will never again be distress and torment, or crying, or agony; for the previous request of things has died" (Disclosure 21:4).

Petition

My dad and my God, I thank you for the Endowment of Jesus to me. Much obliged to you, Master Jesus, for the Endowment of the Essence of God to me. Much obliged to you, Essence of God, for the effortlessness and strength, to come into your presence this second. May the fire, that comes from your presence, purge me, from each messiness, So be it. For the sake of Jesus Christ, and by the force of the Essence of God, any bolt of disorder, influencing my wellbeing, and that of anyone, who is connected with me, by blood, by marriage, and by service, shot from the realm of dimness, by any specialist of Satan, to cause me distress, hardship, and crumbling in my wellbeing, I render you frail, and incapable, So be it. Any wicked bolt of obstinate ailments and hardship, which have resisted prescription, and would not leave me, I reject and criticize you, presently and everlastingly for the sake of Jesus Christ, So be it. For the sake of Jesus Christ, and by the force of the Essence of God, I order and pronounce, that any piece of my body, that is as of now, under evil servitude of ailments, and sicknesses of

any sort, be delivered by fire, be delivered by fire, be delivered by fire. For the sake of Jesus, and by the force of the Essence of God, I order and announce, that nothing more will be tolerated of Satan's torture over my life. I order for the sake of Jesus Christ, that no longer will I [Mention your name], keep on living in affliction and drugs, for the expression of God says in Matthew 4:4, that man will not live by bread alone, however by each word, that emerges, from the mouth of God. My dad and my producer, emerge in your highness, and let your assertion, which is the sword of the Soul, obliterate all that is answerable for the disorders and burdens in my day to day existence this moment, in Jesus' name So be it. In 1 John 3:8, father your statement says, that the explanation Jesus was made manifest, was to annihilate, crafted by Satan in my life. Consequently, you courier of Satan, sent from any evil raised area to torture my wellbeing, [I get beauty, to defeat you, presently and everlastingly in Jesus' name So be it (3times)]. My dad and my creator, I thank you this second, in light of the fact that your assertion says, in Imprint 7:27, that mending is the kids' bread. I'm not an ill-conceived kid, I know, accept and believe that you won't starve, or prevent me from getting my recuperating right presently in Jesus' name So be it. My Ruler Jesus, in your blessed name, I order, that I am presently not wiped out, I'm solid. According to in Joel 3:10, the good book, "let the powerless say, serious areas of strength for i'm". Much thanks to you father for recuperating me, for your promise says in Isaiah 53:5, that "by your injuries, I'm recuperated". In Matthew 8:17, your child Jesus took my sicknesses and bore my illnesses. Subsequently, I order your assertion O Ruler in Galatians 5:1, that opportunity, and not affliction, is what I have, for Christ Jesus has set me free So be it. [In the name Jesus Christ, I proclaim that my life is ablaze for God, and I'm prepared for my recuperating wonder at this moment, So be it (7 times)].

SECTION EIGHT

YOU SHOULD NOT BE MET EMPTY

Why should I not be met empty, Bro. Julius, someone may ask? Beloved, there is dignity in labour. And this was the exact reason why our creator Himself worked.

> *And God saw everything that He had made, and behold, it was very good (suitable, pleasant) and He approved it completely. And there was evening and there was morning; a sixth day. Thus the heavens and the earth were finished, and all the host of them. And on the seventh day God ended His work which He had done; and He rested on the seventh day from all His work which He had done* (Genesis 1:31, 2:1-2 Amplified).

If we are indeed the Bible believing people, the above scriptural verses were particularly written for us to imitate the working character of our creator. But I discovered that a good number of God's people want to imitate what God did on the seventh day only (that's rest). Giving into pleasure has made a lot of people to easily forget that for God to have seen and declared that everything He made were good and rested on the seventh day. He first of all worked hard from day one-to-day six.

Recently, I also realized that my people are not only destroyed by what the Prophet Isaiah and Hosea called ignorance. Nowadays, both the mighty and the small are destroyed in mass daily by pleasure and not by suicide bombers. Beloved, pleasure kills. *"And God saw everything that He had made, and behold, it was very good"*

For things around us to actually have a new nature? We must allow ourselves to be saturated with spiritual, mental and physical works.

Do you know why God told Abram to lift up his eyes from where he was to where He was taking him to (in Genesis 13:14-15)? As a commercial farmer,

You Influence the world

Abram was 99 percent ok as far as physical work is concerned. But when Abram was due for expansion, the first thing God did was to ask him to lift up his eyes from where he was to really see the picture of his future. The significance of that drama between God and Abram, stands for mental capacity building. A lot of people are very much empty nowadays, and this is what leads to great percentage of joblessness which is causing commotion in our society today.

It is time to leave our little beginning and start thinking big. Jesus was born in a manger, and probably had His first meal there. But His last meal was at the upper room that was beautifully decorated. Yes, where you were born is not your choice, but where you will end is your conscious effort and choice. If the physically challenged persons like Helen Keller, who was deaf and dumb was so much addicted to work such that her name was later placed in the anal of history. I'm afraid that if you should allow your destiny or that of the people around you to die because of laziness, anyway I am not God, but I am thinking that you may not escape the place of eternal torment.

Therefore, I charge us to go to work, for even our Lord Jesus Himself was an addicted worker. Yes, I hope you still remember that it took Him a long thirty years of work in preparation for his ministry just for Him to serve humanity for only three years in public ministry? In different occasions, we have seen where the master dismissed the crowd after ministration and still went back to work. In some gospel account, we see statements like "He Prayed All Night". Hello! You can take two minutes break and convince yourself that prayer is work.

Many of us are not standing tall enough for the world to see us today simply because we are too contented with our little last result or accomplishment. We celebrate our last success so much that we fail to paint enough picture of our desired future. Dr. Myles Munroe wrote in one of his books that *"The greatest enemy of your future is your last success".* Beloved, let's follow the pattern of Jesus, for our lord is not only a consuming fire but also a strategic planner. And this was why He never encountered dull moments throughout His public ministry. He was always filled to the brim and was never met empty, not even once.

You Influence the world

If you ask Bartimeus, he would tell you that Jesus simply told him "Go your faith has healed you" (Mark 10:52). If you ask Lazarus of Bethany, he would tell you that he heard Jesus' voice from the land of the dead calling "Lazarus, come out" (John 11:43). If you ask the man who spent thirty eight years at the pool of Bethesda, he would tell you that Jesus told him "Get up! Pick up your mat and walk" (John 5:8). If you ask the hungry multitudes, that were fed by Jesus. They would tell you that even when the apostles told Jesus to send them away on empty stomach, that they simply heard Jesus issue an order for them to sit down in an orderly manner, which made them to eat to their satisfaction and still had left over. If you ask the woman who was caught in the act of adultery, she would tell you that Jesus simply said to her, *"Has no one condemned you? Then neither do I condemn you, go now and leave your life of sin"* (John 8:11). If you ask Zacchaeus the chief tax collector, he would tell you that when Jesus saw him on the top of a tree that He simply said to him, *"Zacchaeus, come down immediately. I must stay at your house today"* (Luke 19:5).If you ask the disciples that traveled with Jesus on that day that the storm rose against them. They would tell you that the master simply said to the waves "Quiet! Be Still" (Mark 4:39). In the gospel of John (9:4) our Lord Himself expressly said "We must work the works of Him who sent me and be busy with His business while it is daylight; night is coming on when no man can work" (Amplified).

As a child of God, it is an undeniable responsibility to work and we should not be met empty. For even the master Himself said in the above scripture that work is a necessity while it is daylight. Having read this, I know someone may ask, Brother Julius, when am I expected to do this work you are talking about? Well, the answer is simple. As far as the grace of God is still upon you, the work continues. *"[Growing in grace] they shall still bring forth fruit in old age; they shall be full of sap [of spiritual vitality] and [rich in the] verdure [of trust, love, and contentment Psalm 92:14 Amplified]".*

In the parable of the ten virgins, the five foolish ones were shut out of the wedding feast because of their emptiness. They really missed it because the time they ought to have used to gather extra oil for their lamps was used for frivolities and other things that did not count. They were called foolish and totally disqualified for not staying at the appropriate field they were called to cultivate. *"The lord God took the man, and put him in the garden to work it and take care of it"* (Genesis 2:15 Niv).

Our attitude to work is the very reason why many people who were created to be world changers are still stagnant today. Beloved, pleasure kills. Should you be among those who are crazy about movies and sports, I am not against it but please permit me to also ask you this question; how many times has Christiano Ronaldo of Portugal, Leonel Messi of Argentina, Olu Jacob and Pet Edochie of Nigeria, Under-Taker and John Cena of America abandoned the rigorous training that are associated with the area of their expertise to come to your shop or office to watch how you run your affairs for hours? Sincerely, I am not against sports and movies, as I said earlier, I watch them during leisure. But my point here is that we should learn how to prioritize and consciously give to Caesar exactly what belongs to him and to our God what belongs to Him.

Your inability to discover where you were wired in life is the reason for your emptiness. Infact, even if you were born out of wedlock or at a time your parents said they were above the age for child baring, I want you to know that you are not an accident. Instead, you are fully in the number of those that God beautifully brought into this world to make impact.

In the gospel of Mathew (25:14-30) we saw an account, were three servants were given different kinds of gifts by their master. Two among the three, two had a clear understanding and the implication of one being empty and decided to go to work without delay. While they were busy investing what was impacted on them by their master, the other lazy and wicked servant was met empty. Why? Instead of using his own gift like his colleagues, he went and buried his gift and chose to gossip and complain over the things he had no power to control. If you have discovered your gift, and you are exactly doing what God has called you to do, hardly will you have free time because at this level, your major concern will be how I will improve my character and skill so that lives will be more blessed through my gift and work. *"So David fed them according to the integrity of his heart; and guided them by the skillfulness of his hands"* (Psalm 78:72).

You Influence the world

It is emptiness, laziness and lack of work that leads people mainly into covetousness, gossip and unhealthy competition. And every unhealthy competition is as a result of mission diverted. Dr (Pastor) Paul Enenche said, and I quote, *"The desire to be like everybody, is the reason for many nobodies"* And Raph Waldo Emerson also said and I quote, *"to be yourself in a world that is constantly trying to make you something else is the greatest accomplishment".*

Beloved, if you fail to discover, develop and utilize your gift, rest assured that no amount of excuses will stop the Master from calling you the same name He called that empty fellow in Mathew (25:26) ("You Wicked and Lazy Slave" on the Day of Judgment) and please don't be quick to forget the following statement by Saint Paul, *"Therefore, you have no excuse whoever you are"* (Romans 2:1A).

In Genesis chapter 11, all the people in that community were so much addicted to work such that it took God's intervention only to stop them from building an outstanding tower that would have reached the sky. Hear me, if you decide today to work out your salvation with fear and trembling (Phillipians2:12), I can assure you that like a moving train, you are unstoppable until you reach your station. If you are not yet connected to that position you are looking forward to, don't relent, but continue to get yourself prepared, for a day shall come when your preparation shall meet with your opportunity and you will be so surprise that the same people who belittled you in the past, will come back to you with their silver and gold, tears and invitation.

> *"Then his brothers also wept, fell down before him, and said, we are here as slaves. But Joseph said to them do not be afraid! Am i in the place of God? Even though you intended to do harm to me, God intended it for good, in order to preserve a numerous people, as he is doing today"* (Genesis 50:18-20).

The Master, and the Fruitless Fig Tree.

Folks, I don't know about you, but I have seen some people who are blindly backing up their emptiness with the fact that the Bible records that "Vanity upon vanity all is vanity" but these people who base their argument on the above quote, seem to be unaware maybe because of ignorance that after that particular verse, the next verse also said that the same man who made that comment of *"vanity upon vanity"* also sought knowledge, wrote and organized many proverbs (Ecclesiastes 12:9).

Is it not laughable and disheartening that the same set of people, who have vehemently refused to get themselves fixed into work that will make them respond to their responsibilities, but chose to sing the song of "vanity upon vanity" still expect their family and friends to carry their daily loads at forty? Just imagine someone who neither has a skill or a certificate that could get him a better job, yet he wants his aging parents to marry a wife for him, so he can continue to raise a generation of destitutes. I once had a contact with this kind of person, who had given birth to ten children and had no defined plan on how to take care of those children. I was shocked when I heard that man deferring his responsibility to God by saying that it is God that trains children. Folks, this is unacceptable and wrong, it is this kind of understanding that leads into a complete loss of sense of responsibility. Sincerely, we are not right at all if we continue to claim that we love God and yet fail to demonstrate our love for Him by first loving the responsibility He gave us.

In the gospel of Mark chapter 11, Jesus was totally disappointed with the fig tree simply because it looked fruitful from afar, but when He went closer to it so that He can at least enjoy its fruitfulness, He realized that it was fruitless. The greatest form of deception is camouflage, which is a result of not telling oneself the truth. For instance, if that fig tree did not live a pretentious life, it wouldn't have incurred Jesus' anger.

The dendrologist would tell you that for fig trees, the fruit appears at the same time as the leaves. So it simply means that the nutrient that the unproductive fig tree sapped from the earth was also enough for it to bear fruits. Now, if one is not careful enough while reading that drama between Jesus and that fruitless fig tree, one maybe tempted to quickly question Jesus authority of cursing that tree since it was not it's the season. We must take note that Jesus is the master and therefore

His authority and actions must not for any reason be questioned. Do you know why? First, He is the Wisdom personified. Second, we must also learn that if it is not yet time for us to manifest, we are expected to be ourselves and continue to dig deeper; such that when we are finally revealed, the expectation of the creation which eagerly await our manifestation will not be disappointed. Third, we must note that if Jesus did not see leaves on that fruitless fig tree, He wouldn't have gone closer to it in the first place.

Dream Big

Dreams are ideal in achieving goals toward which one aspires. That particular thing we so desire to be in the future. As a matter of fact, anyone who desires to succeed in the race of life must be a dreamer. In several cases we have seen people from humble background excelling and doing the impossible in their field because of the power of dream. Dream is a motivator. We really need to have big dreams because if our dream (vision) is only equivalent to the resources at our disposal, we will only accomplish little or end our mission prematurely.

Recently, a group of believers were asked what I call a big question during a seminar, and that is, *"Where do they see themselves in thirty years time"?* This kind of question is so crucial, because a lot of people are seriously wasting their resources on feasting when they ought to be saving or fasting for the future. When God blessed the entire universe with extraordinary resources (blessings) before that great famine, men and women who did not see the future were busy eating up resources that were meant for the future. *"Where there is no vision, the people perish"* (Proverb 29:18 AMP). When you have a big dream, your mind will be stretched beyond limitation, and once your mind is opened, you will be motivated to display a commitment far beyond your mandate.

Beloved, if you are going to make your big dream a reality, you need to associate with people who dreamt big and achieved their dreams. I hope you have not forgotten the saying that, *"birds of the same feather, flock together"*. If you accept my charge to have a big dream so that you can move forward in life, then you must avoid close association with a group of people I call, "*Road Blocks to Success*". In other words, your association will either make or mar you. Among these fellows I called *"road block to success"* are some who never dreamt for once, others dreamt little but were not able to achieve what they dreamt of, while others really dreamt big and even pursued it, but gave up when they had almost achieved their dream.

In Genesis chapter 41, Pharaoh had a dream which later made him and his kingdom the centre of attraction around the globe, because when he had the dream, he left his daily routine saying *'NO'* to all the commoners around him, and summoned Joseph the dreamer who the Bible tells us had the excellent Spirit and loved God above all things (Genesis 39:9).

REFERENCES

Bill Splendid, @ (1999). "God: Find His Character."Published by New Life Distributions, A service of Grounds Campaign for Christ. P.O. Box 620877, Orlando, FL 328620877.

David O. Oyedepo, @ (1995). "Satan Get Lost." Distributed in Nigeria by: Territory Distributing House, km 10, Idiroko Street, Canaan Land, Ota, Nigeria.

Gloria Copeland, @ (2010). "Live lengthy, End on a positive note." Imprinted in the US of America.

Fire up. Fr. Uche Stephen Njoku, "Then came Jesus." Distributed by Christian Living Distribution Service, Second story Room Services, 18 Aria Rd. G.R.A. P.O. Box 17860 Enugu, Enugu State Nigeria. Telephone: 042-256512.

Gordon Lindsay, @ (2001). "Charged with Power - an outline of the gifts of the Essence of God." Distributed under consent from Christ for the Countries Inc, in Nigeria by Evangel Distributers Ltd.

Kenneth E. Hagin @ (1999). "Book of scriptures Recuperating Concentrate Course". Imprinted in USA by Kenneth Hagin Services, Inc.

Kenneth E. Hagin, @ (1997). "The Recuperating Blessing". Imprinted in USA.

Most Fire up. Dr. Felix Alaba (1998), "Catholic Song Book" Distribute by St. Pauls, Printed by SAP print arrangement Pvt. Ltd 28, Lakshmi indusial bequest, SN way, lower parel (w) Mumbai.

Roberts Liardon, @ (2011). "GOD'S Commanders: The Recuperating Evangelist."Printed in the US of America by Roberts Liardon.

Roberts Liardon, @ (2009). "John G. Lake on Recuperating." Imprinted in US of America.

Smith Wigglesworth On Recuperating @ (1999). Distributed under authorization from Whitaker House in Nigeria by Evangel Distributers Ltd.

The Blessed Book of scriptures (New Modified Standard Variant). This release @ 2008 the English and unfamiliar Book of scriptures Society assets Ltd. Imprinted in China.

T.L. Osborn, @ (2004). "Message that works."Printed in USA by LaDonna Osborn.

www.ingramcontent.com/pod-product-compliance
Lightning Source LLC
LaVergne TN
LVHW050337160826
845677LV00014B/3663

* 9 7 9 8 3 7 8 3 7 0 8 4 9 *